SWITCHED ON

PUNCH on Television

Edited by William Hewison

A PUNCH BOOK
Published in association with
GRAFTON BOOKS
A Division of the Collins Publishing Group

LONDON GLASGOW
TORONTO SYDNEY AUCKLAND

Grafton Books
A Division of the Collins Publishing Group
8 Grafton Street, London W1X 3LA

Published by Grafton Books 1987

British Library Cataloguing in Publication Data

Switched on: Punch on television
1. Television – Caricatures and cartoons
2. English wit and humor, Pictorial
I. Hewison, William
741.5'942 NC1476

ISBN 0-246-13174-8

Printed in Great Britain by
William Collins Sons Ltd, Westerhill, Glasgow

Introduction

It's on the cards that I might have missed a page or two during my researches but I'm pretty confident that the first cartoon about television to appear in *Punch* featured a broadcast of a mixed-doubles tennis match. Direct from Ceylon. Live. The cartoonist who produced this jokey landmark was that master of the cross-hatch, George du Maurier, and the date his piece of penwork reached the printed page was not, as you might think, 1929, the year the BBC first sent out its flickering images on to the air waves, but 1878, a set of numbers not usually linked with the invention of the goggle box.

Du Maurier's drawing has the tennis match on a wide screen above the mantelpiece in an English home, and whereas it proves the artist to be quite a dab hand at prophesying that eventually we'd have John McEnroe's half-volleys bounced into our living-rooms from far-off Los Angeles, George didn't get the name of this extraordinary device quite right. He called it 'Edison's Telephonoscope' – a forgivable error in the circumstances, as any Logie Bairds around at that time were probably back there in Dumbartonshire baking bannocks or hunting the haggis.

We now know, of course, that the Scotsman beat the American (and all others) to it, and subsequently his nifty invention has not only driven many a man out to the pub of an evening, but has given the world's cartoonists a steady source for their drolleries. The standard themes are trotted out frequently – the regular programmes, the techniques of studio production, the television sets on the blink, the advertisements, the personalities – but most regular of all is the response of him and her to that thing lurking in the corner of the room. And from time to time throughout the years the cartoonist is helped along by way of the changes and developments which have come on stream, such as the arrival of Commercial TV, and Colour, and Remote Controls, in each case providing him with a fresh patch to dig over.

However, there is a tiny problem which the cartoonist has difficulty in avoiding: so many of his ideas require nothing more than a drawing of a TV set and a couple of people watching it, which, let's face it, can become a bit repetitious. He can also occasionally get into a rut with his ideas, whereby he turns out (say) yet another variation on the subject of Repeat Programmes. Fortunately, in a collection like this one it is possible to pick and choose a more balanced mixture, one which takes account of all aspects and underlines the fact that *Punch* cartoonists, where TV is concerned, have always been switched on.

William Hewison

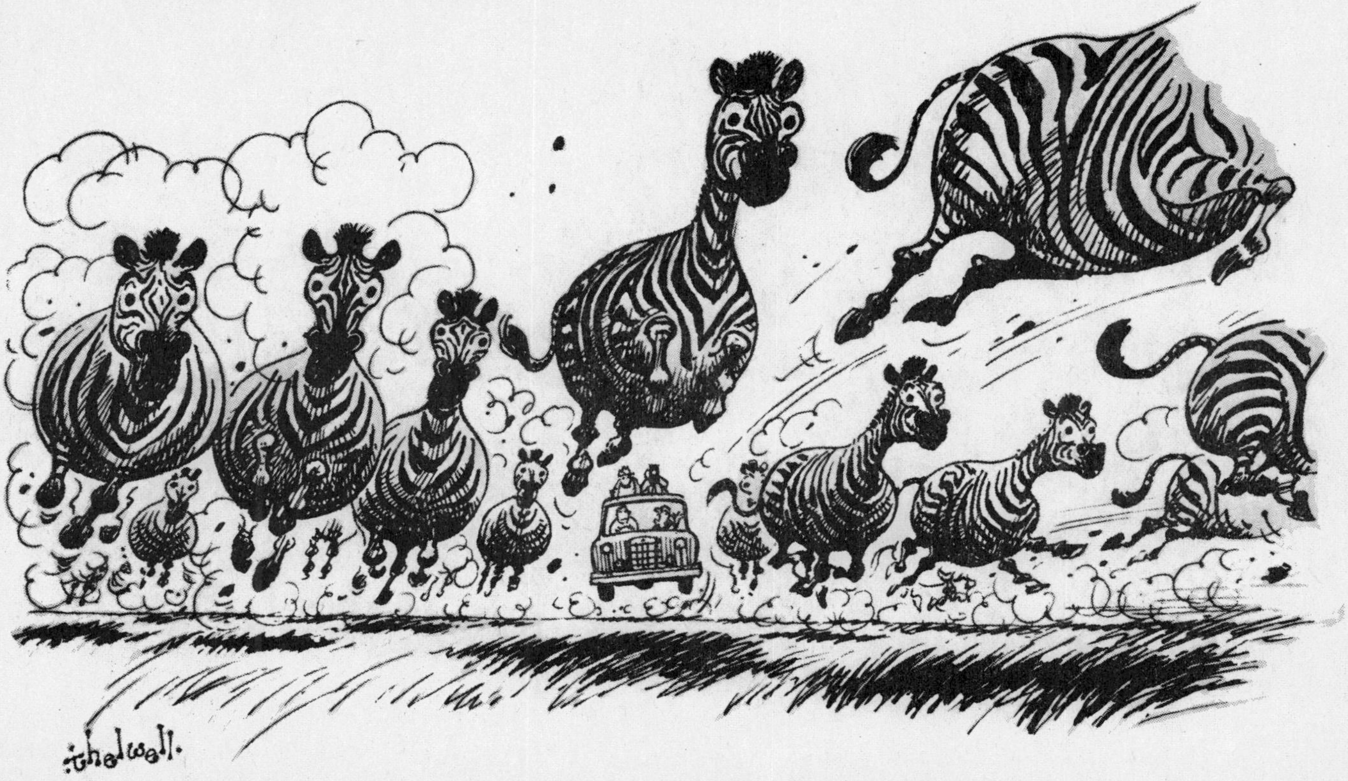

*"It's good television! But is it good **colour** television?"*

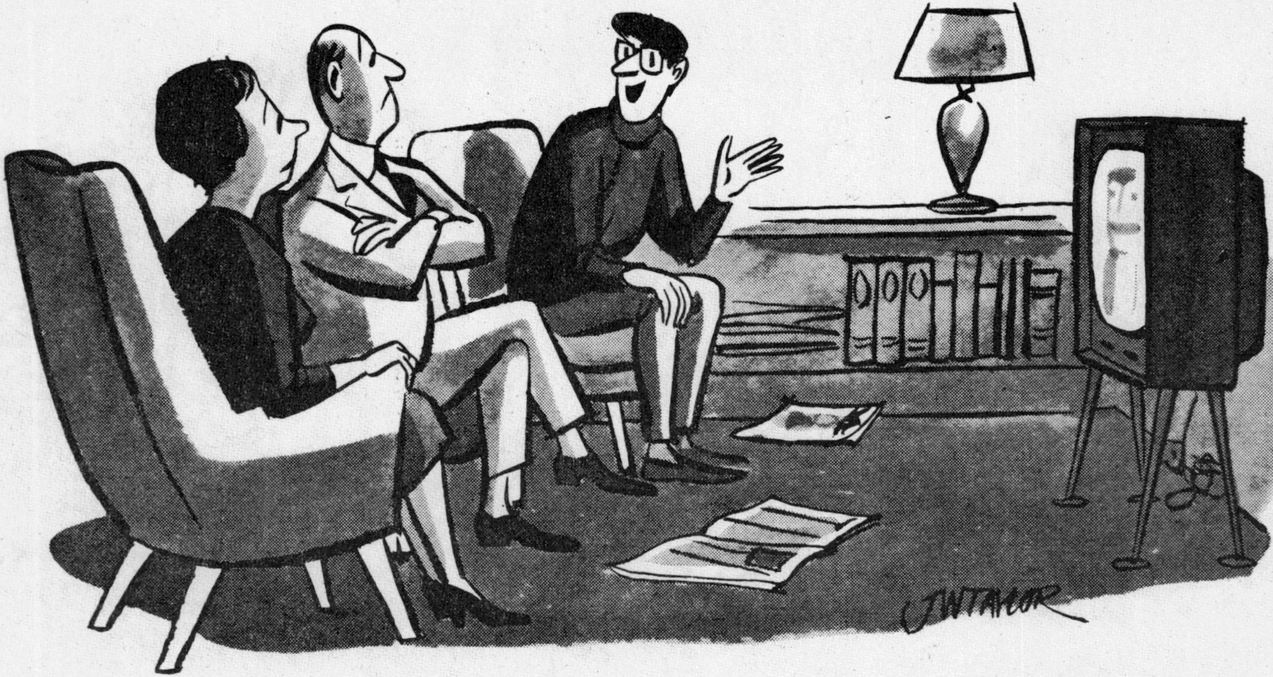

"Get it? It's a skit on the programme that did a send-up of the show that took the mickey out of this series."

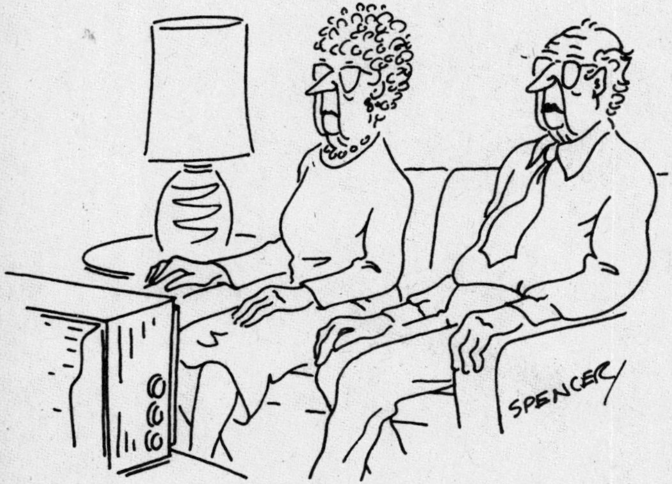

"Jimmy Stewart is looking really old these days . . ."

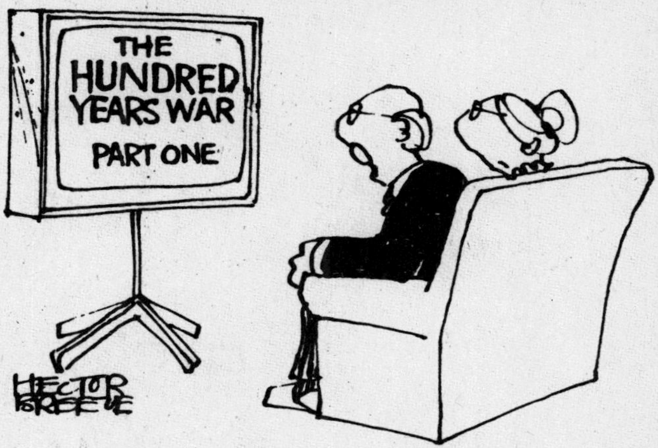

"Well, let's just see as many episodes as we can."

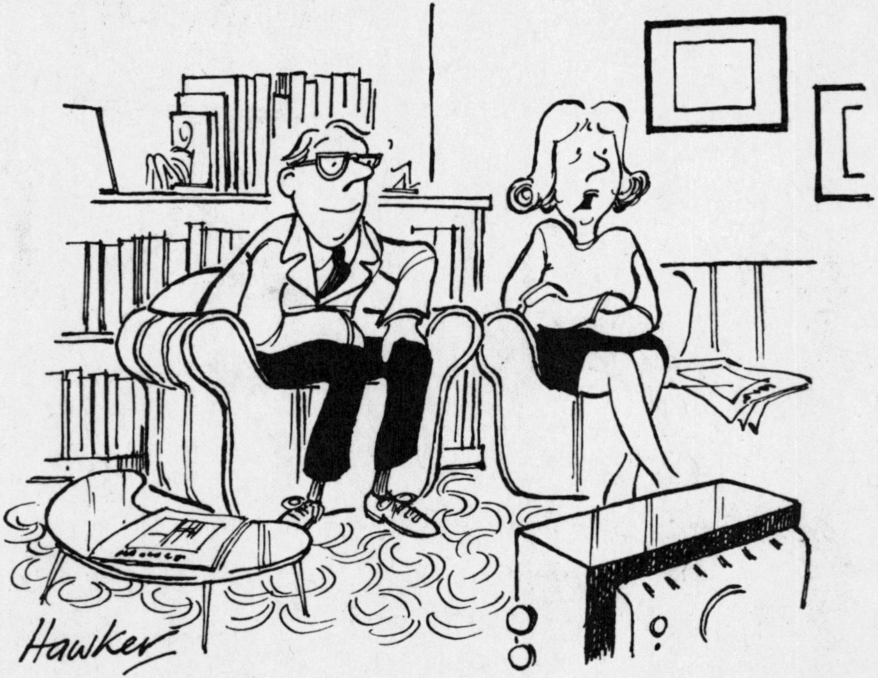

"You realise this is working class humour you're laughing at?"

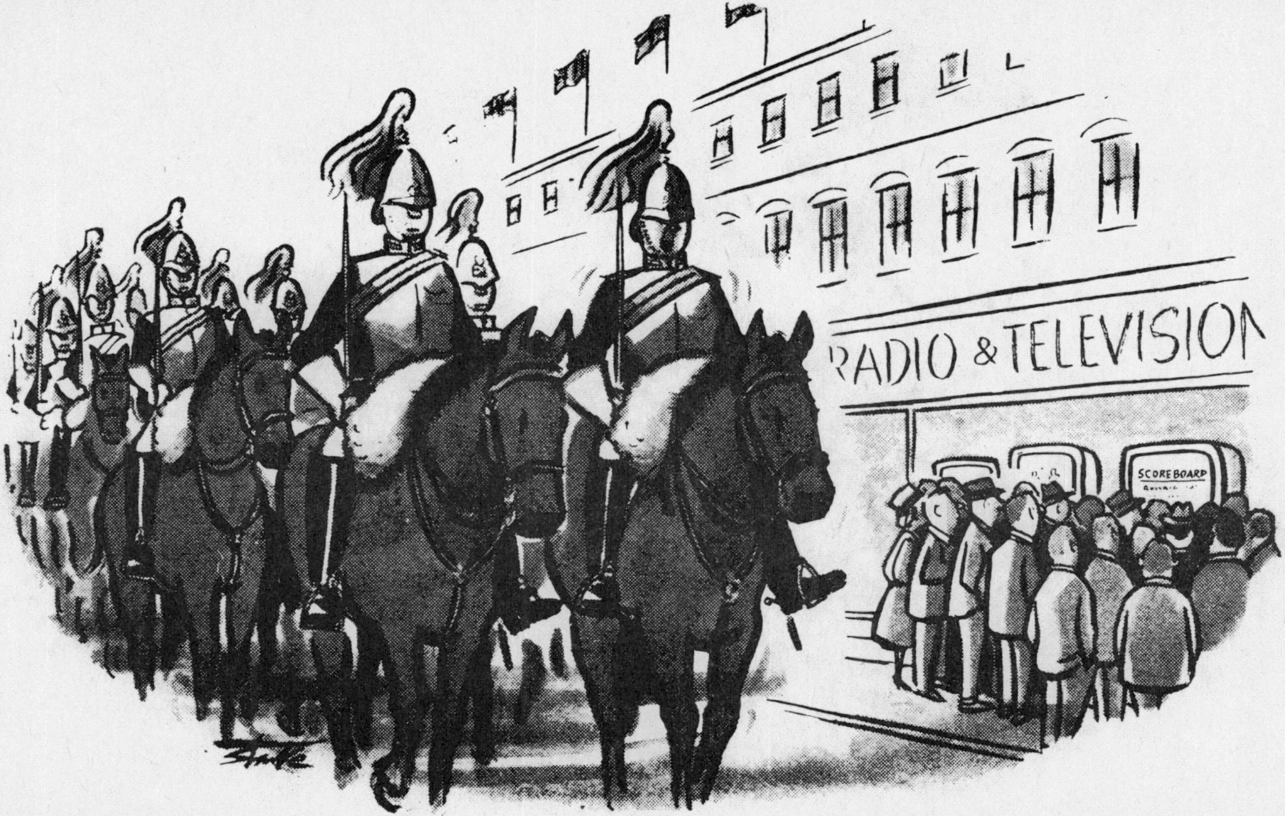

"Ninety-two for four."

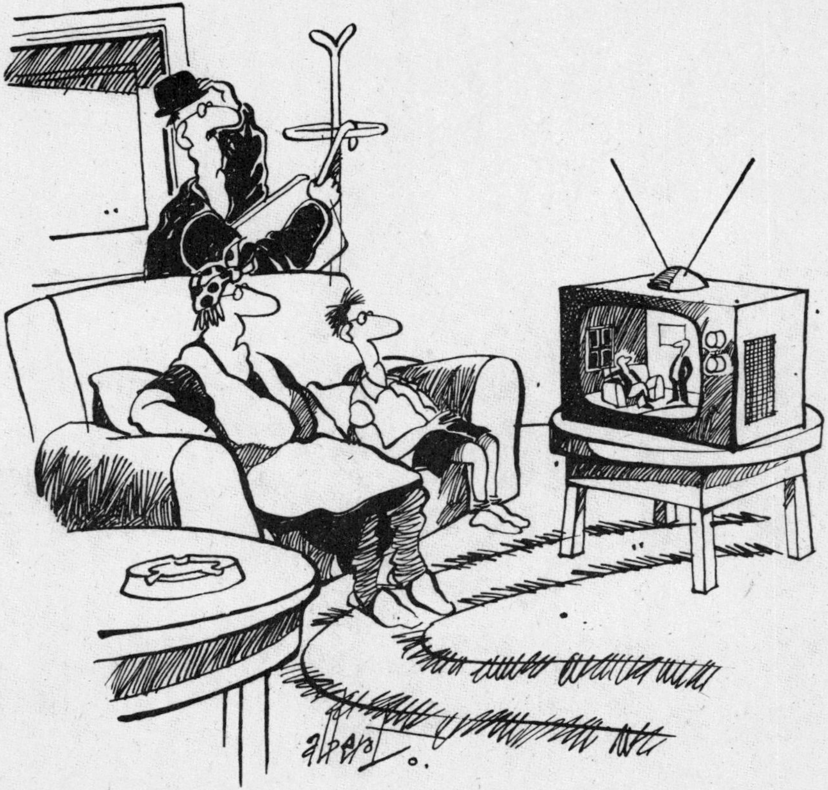

"Put the Western on, son – your dad's been stuck inside all day."

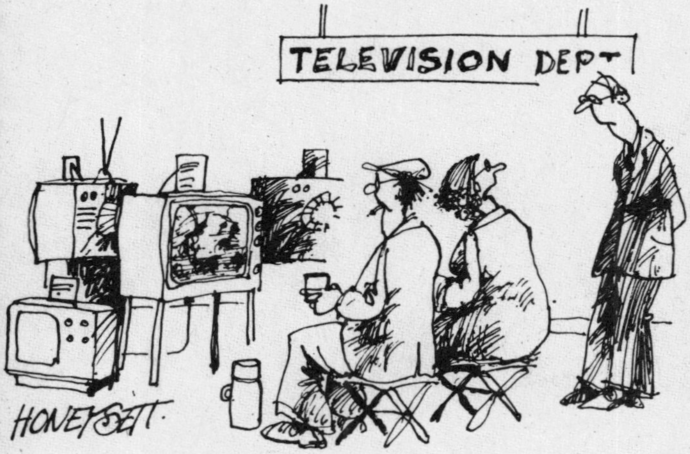

"No thanks, we're just looking."

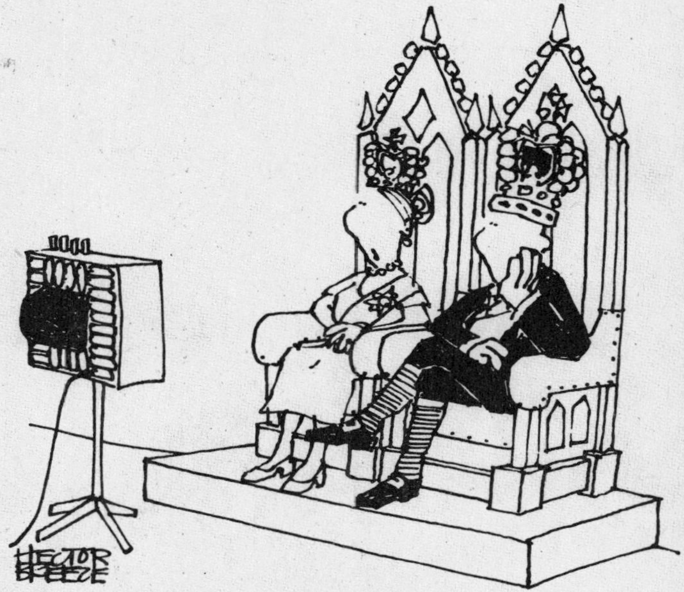

"You always think they're worse than you remembered them from the Royal Film Performance."

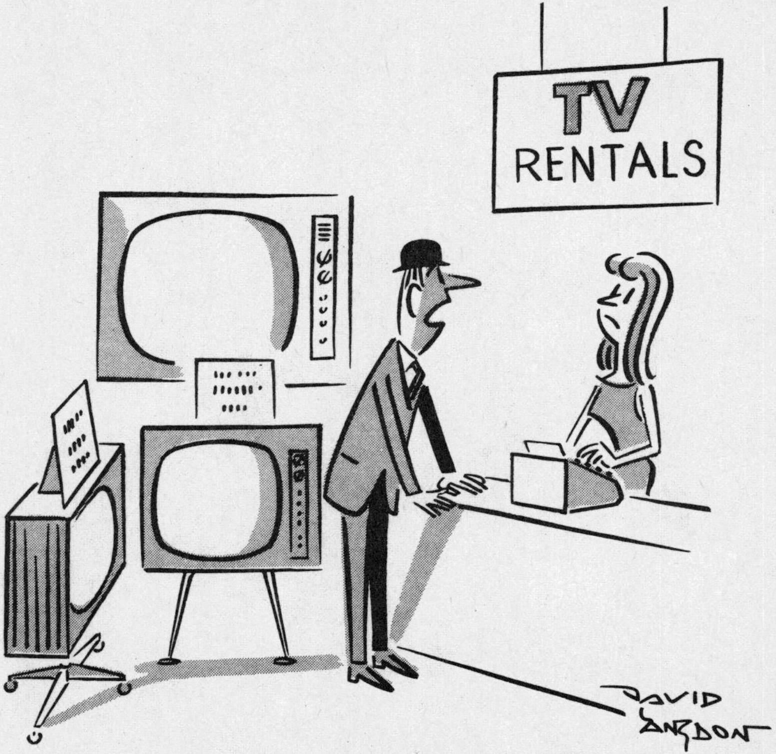

"Any refund if we give it up just for the October Party Conferences?"

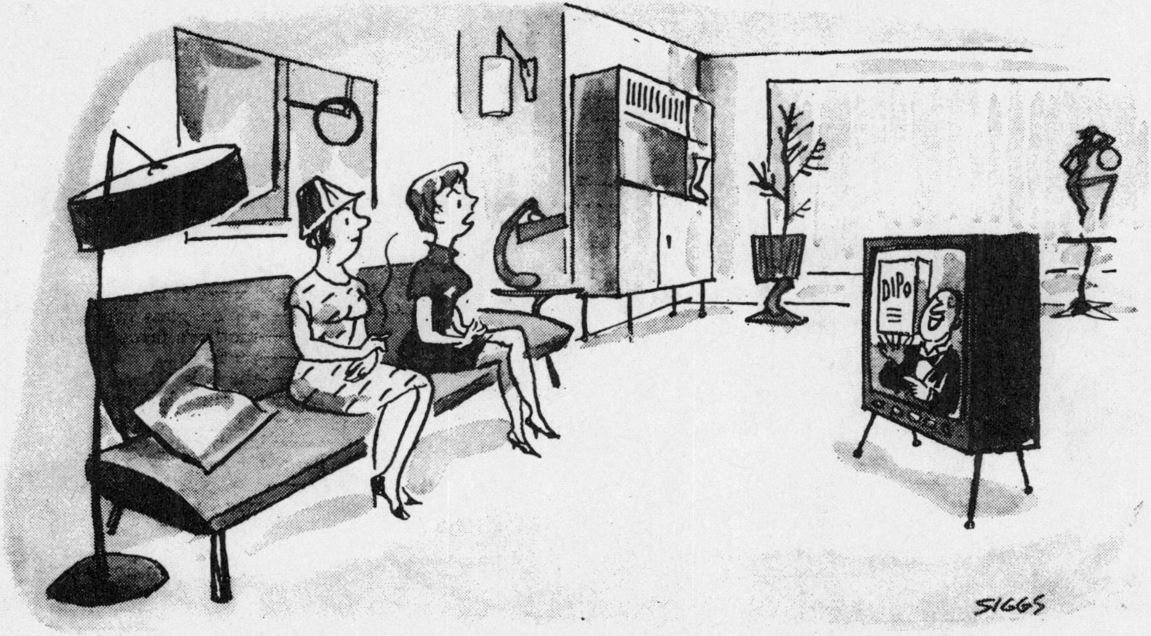

"I shall have to stop buying it or be accused of falling for TV advertising."

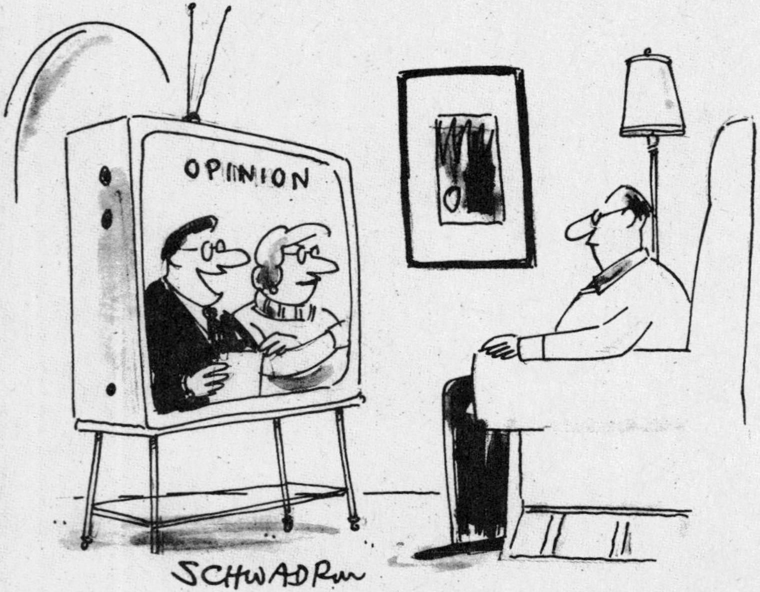

"Now, for an opposing viewpoint, here's my wife."

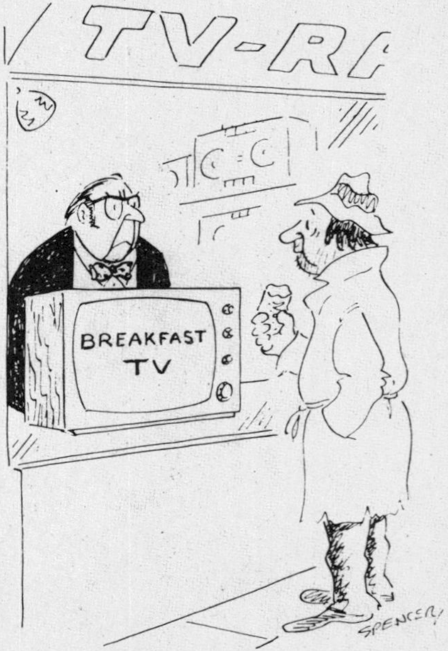

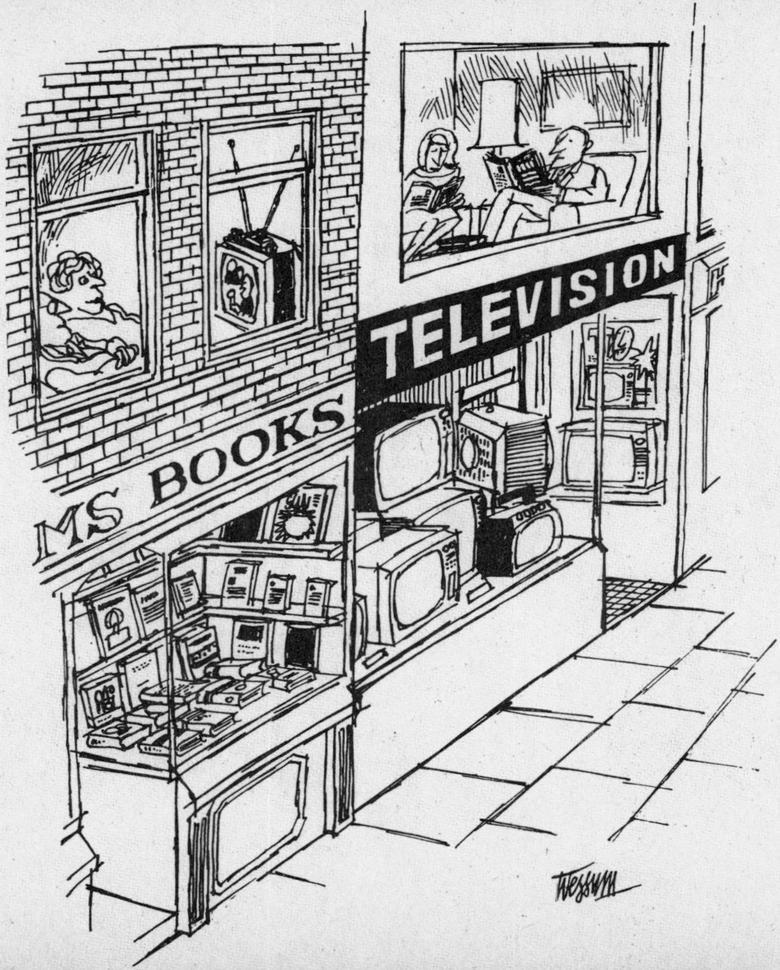

MS BOOKS
TELEVISION

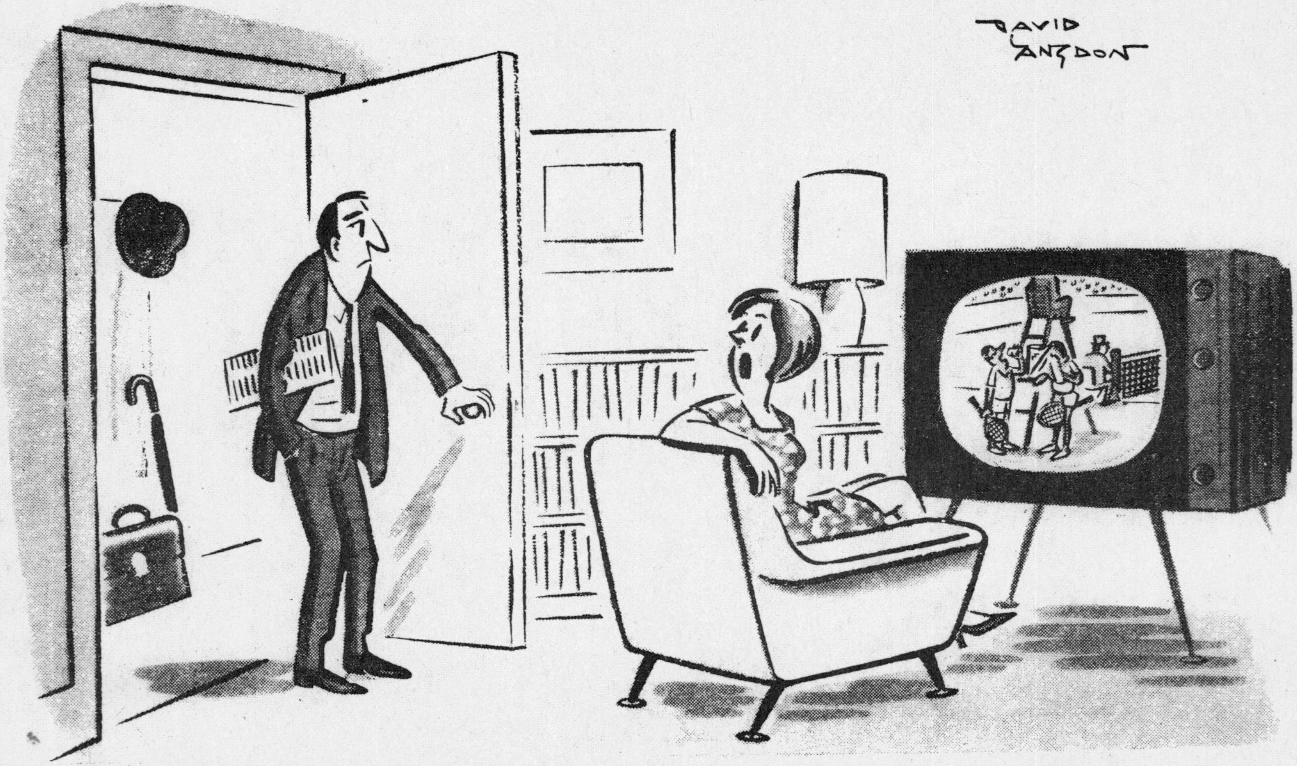

"Cold meat in larder, lettuce in fridge, tomatoes in shopping bag on kitchen door – quickly now!"

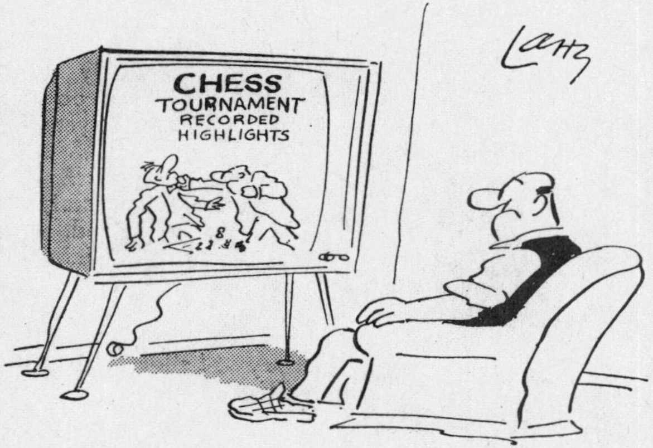

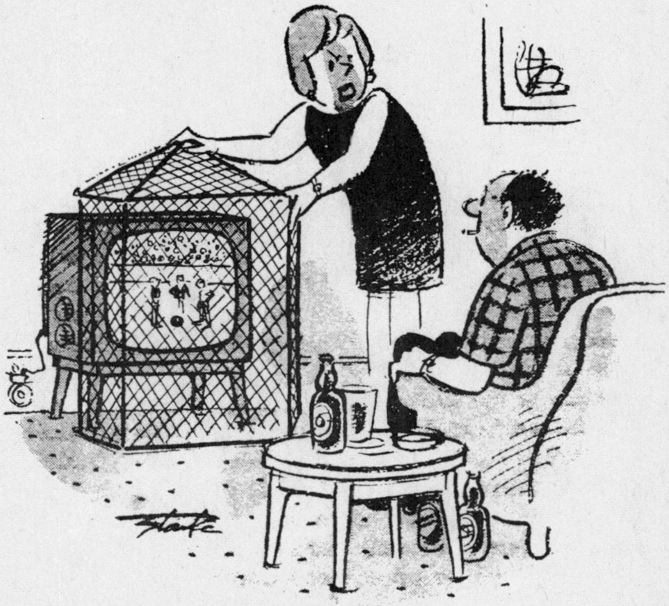

"Well, you know what a hooligan you
can be when you get excited."

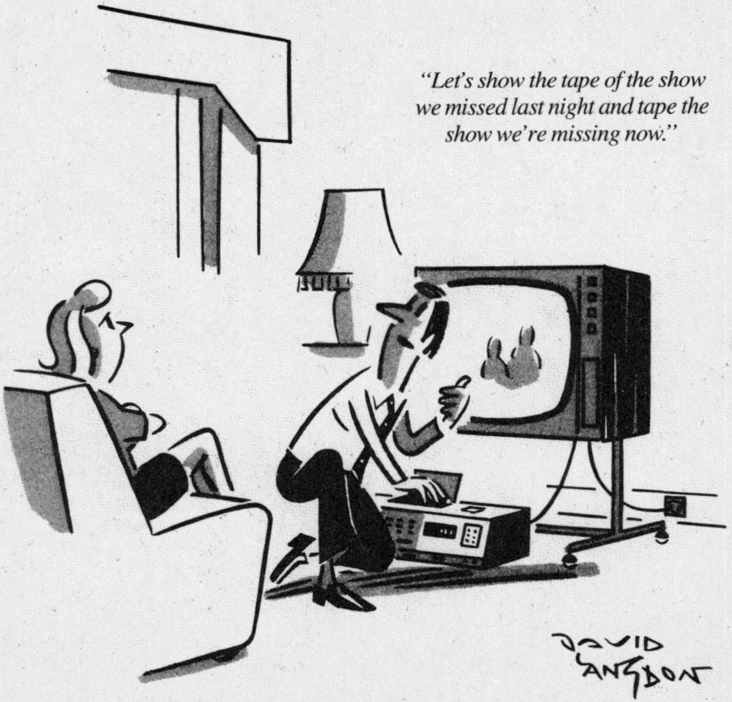

"Let's show the tape of the show we missed last night and tape the show we're missing now."

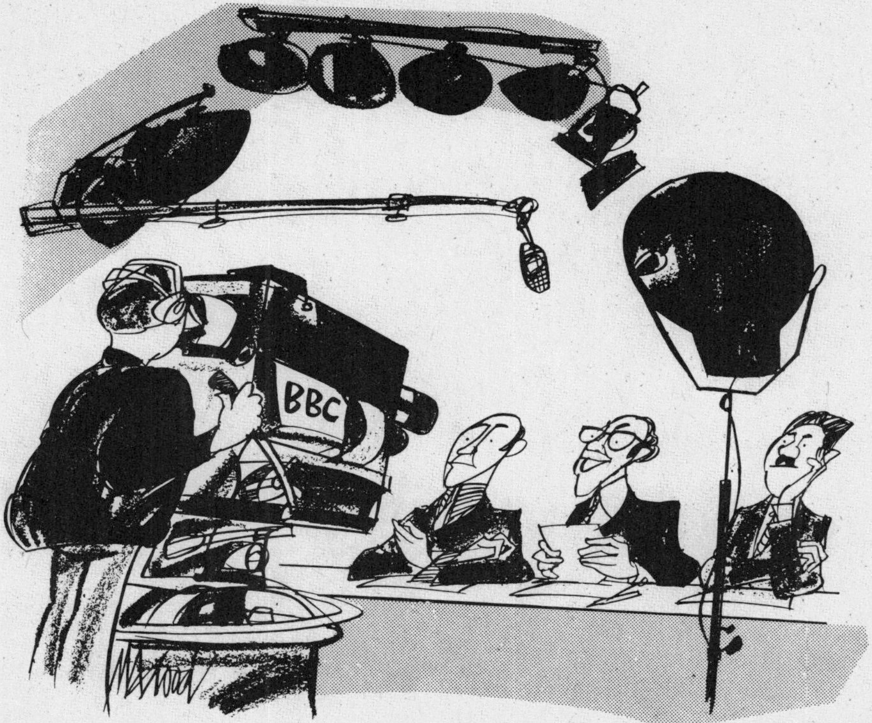

". . . and at the end of our discussion of the Chancellor's new measures, an independent expert will assess the degree of bias shown."

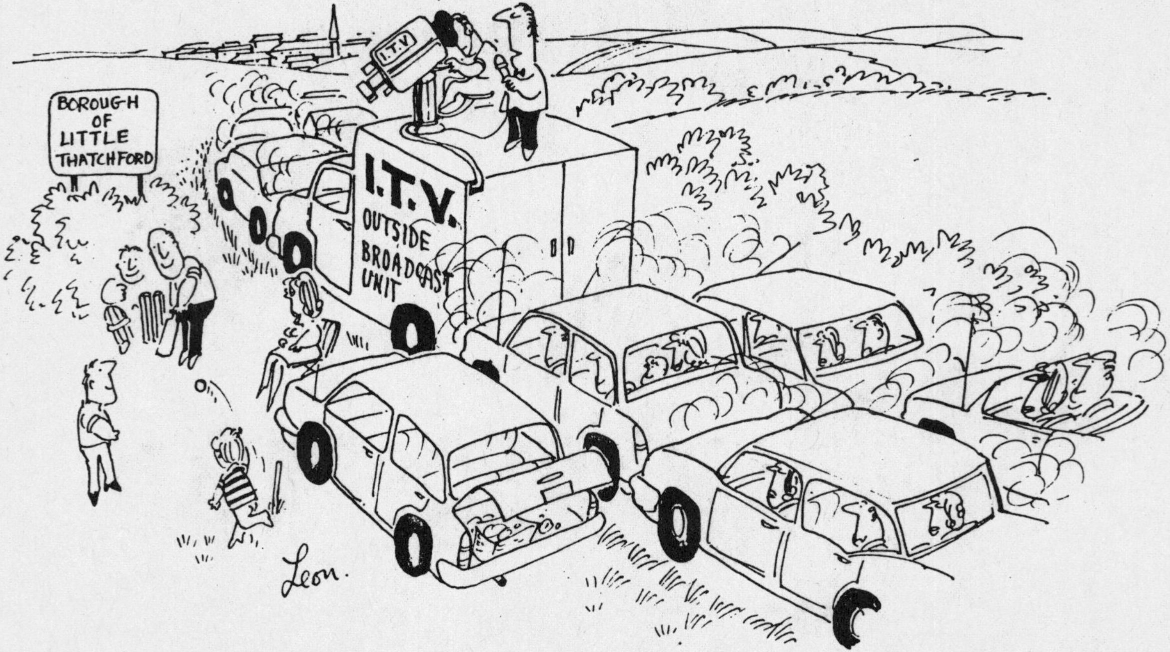

"We have a change in our afternoon programme. And instead of racing from Newmarket, we are covering cricket from Little Thatchford!"

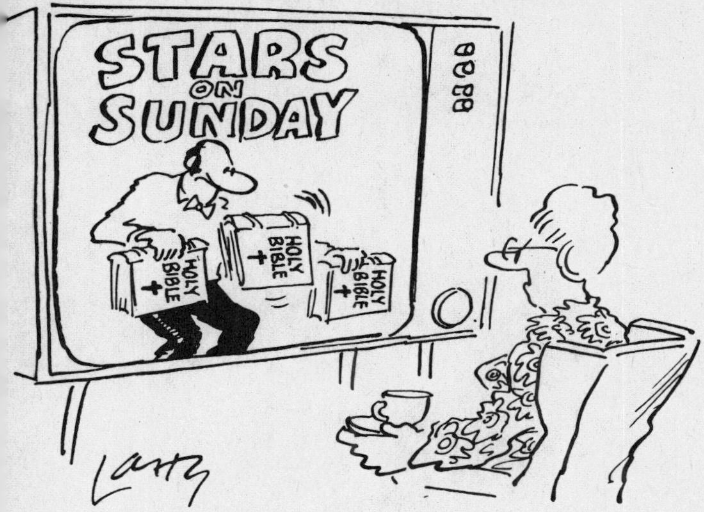

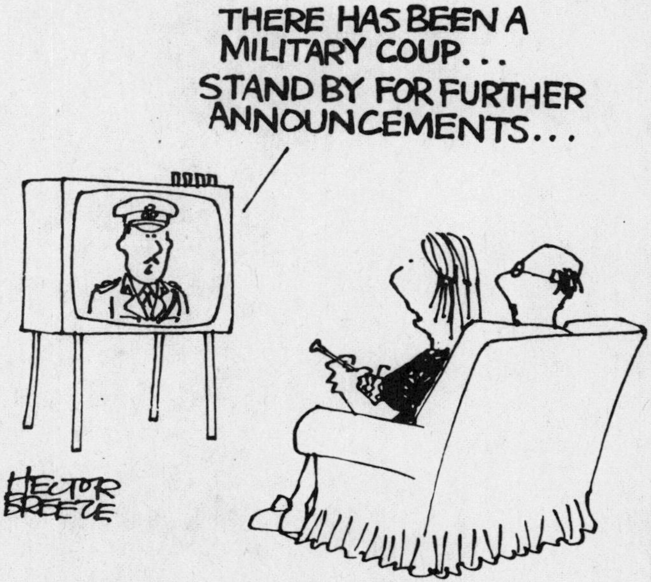

"Isn't he the one who played Mr. Whatshisname in that serial on Tuesdays?"

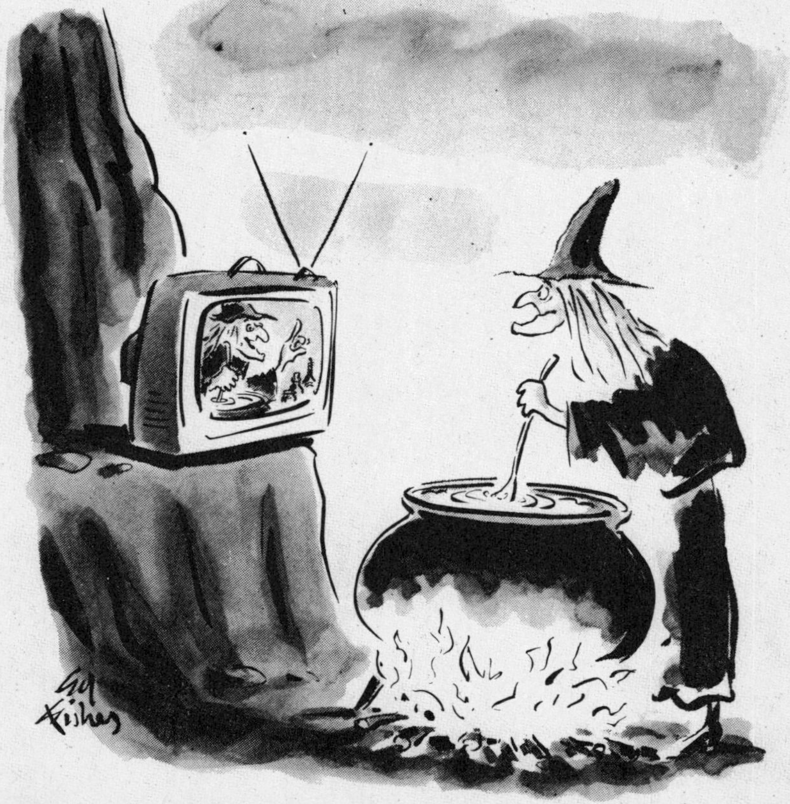
Ed Fisher

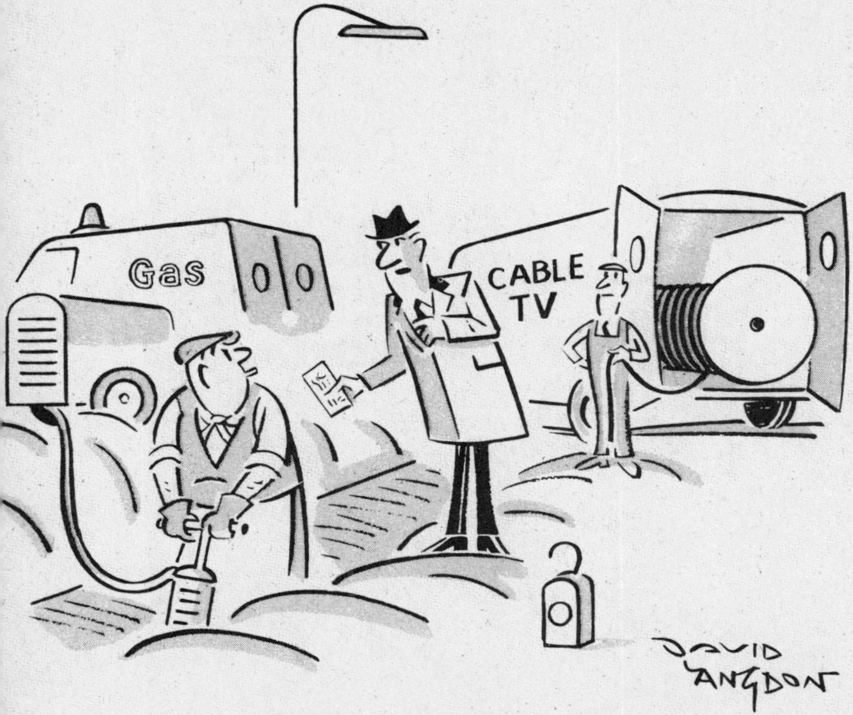

"Any chance of slipping us in while you're at it?"

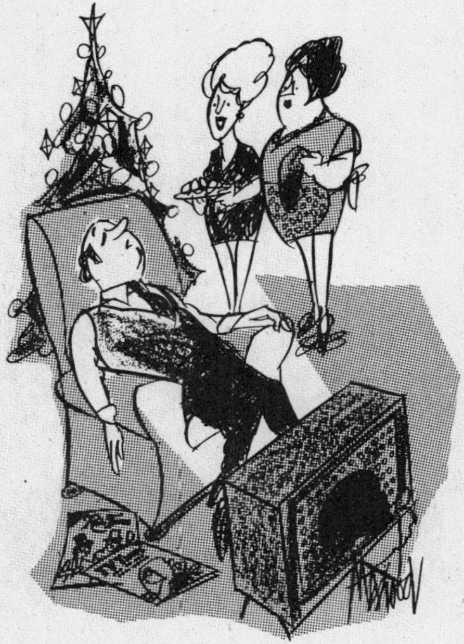

"I think it's a draw – BBC made him switch over and ITV has put him to sleep."

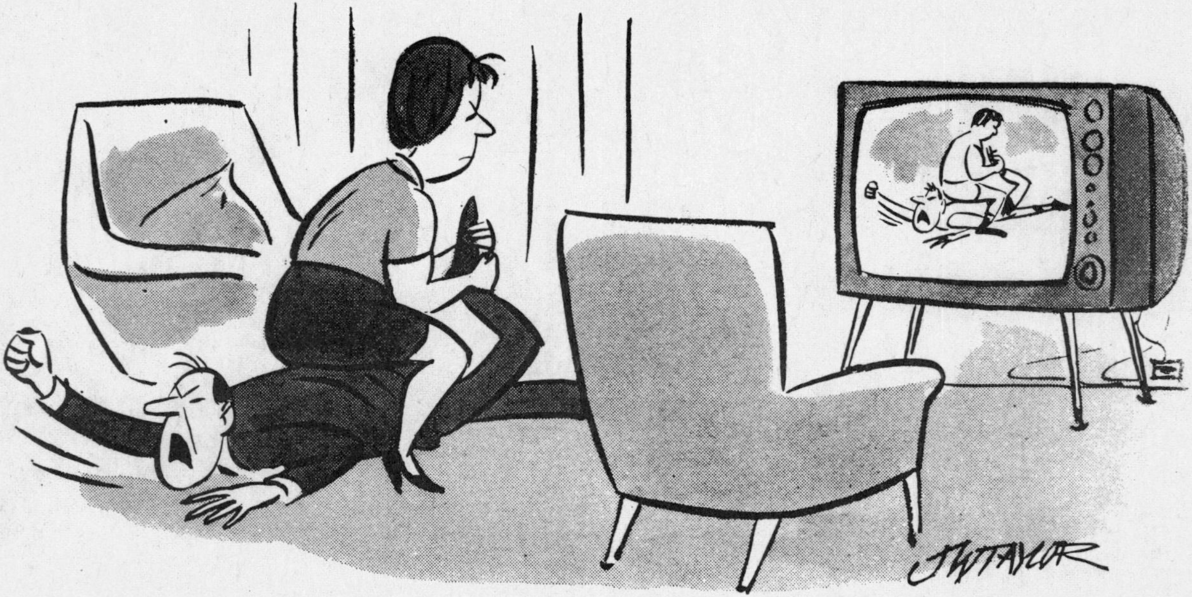

"All right, all right – he **isn't** overacting . . ."

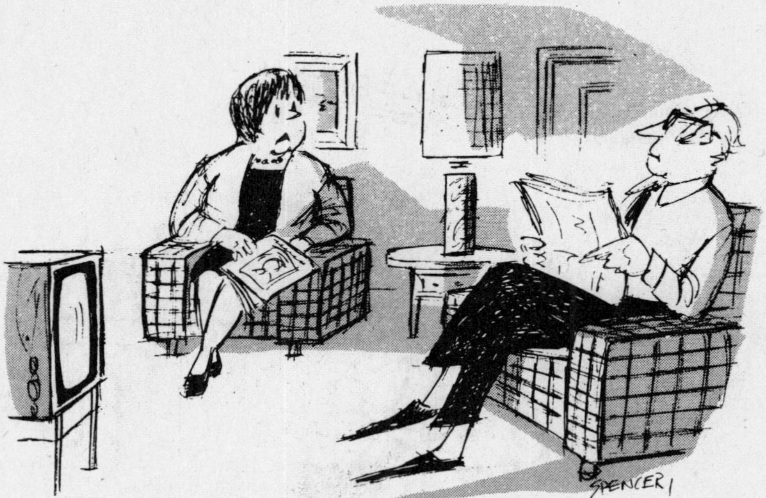

"But Arthur, we can't sit here at peak viewing time and not watch ***something****!"*

"Do you think that perhaps David Coleman is past his personal best?"

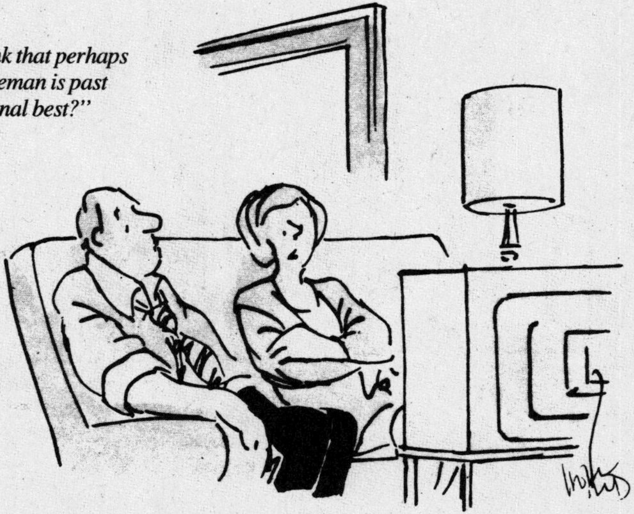

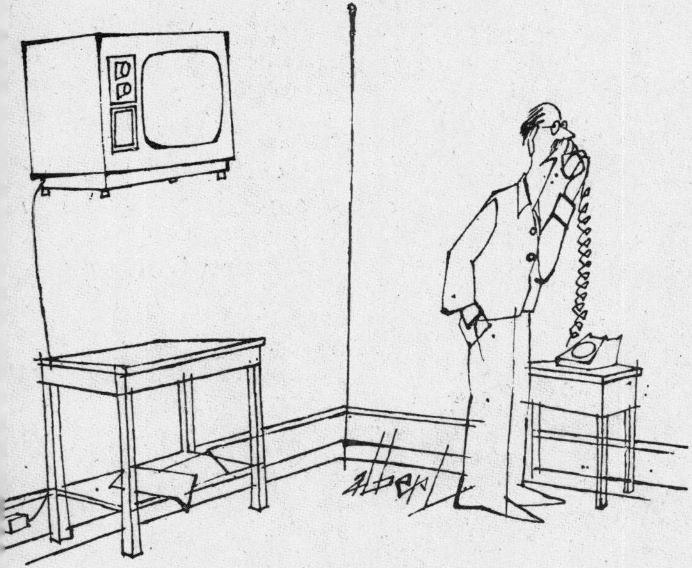

"It's the vertical hold."

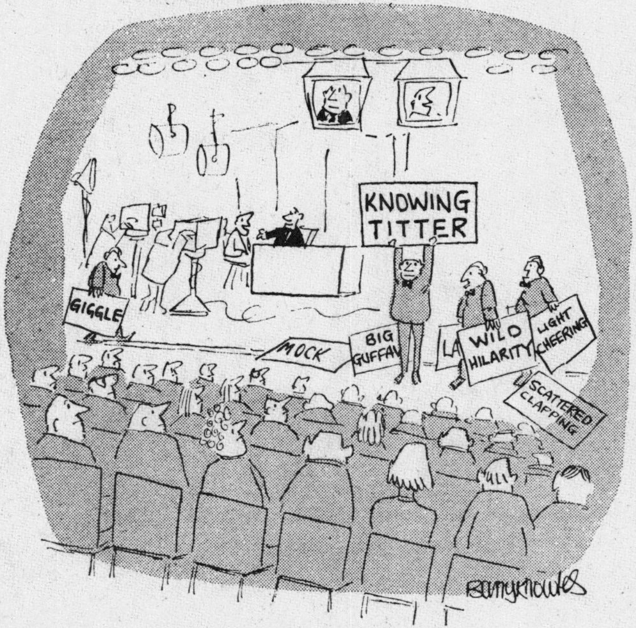

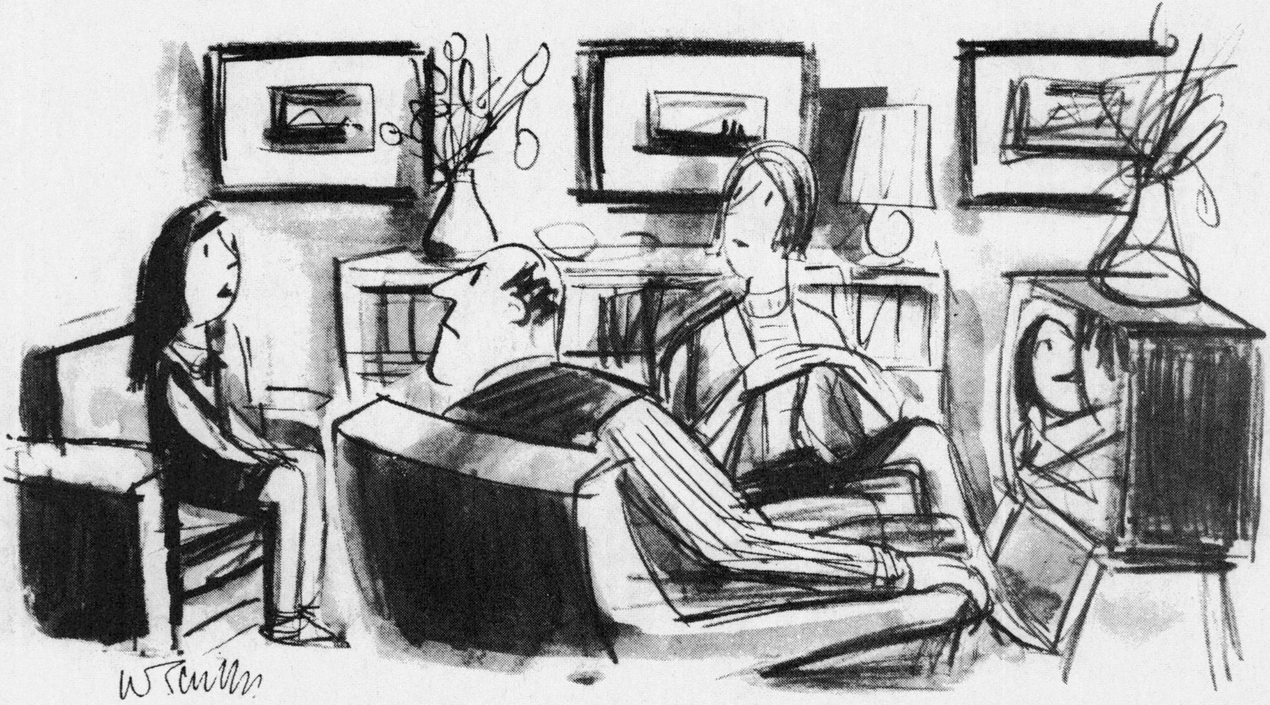

"If it's sex, I'd better stay up and watch it – we're bound to be asked a question about it at school tomorrow."

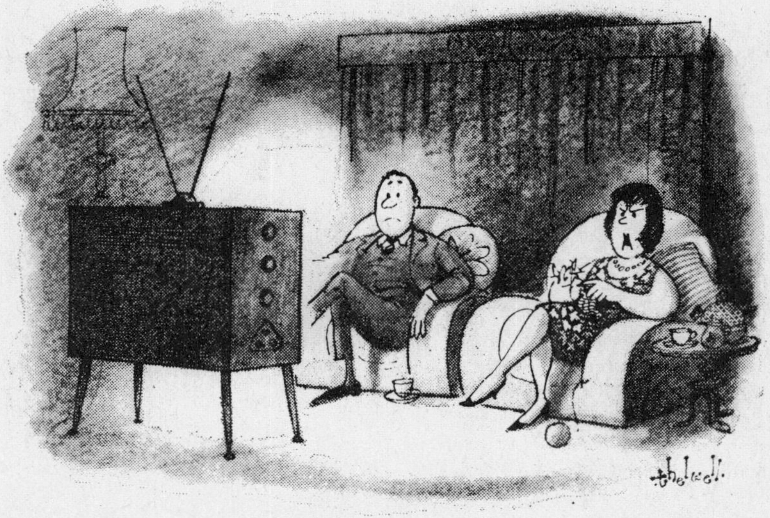

"It needs adjusting. They should go blue when they're strangled."

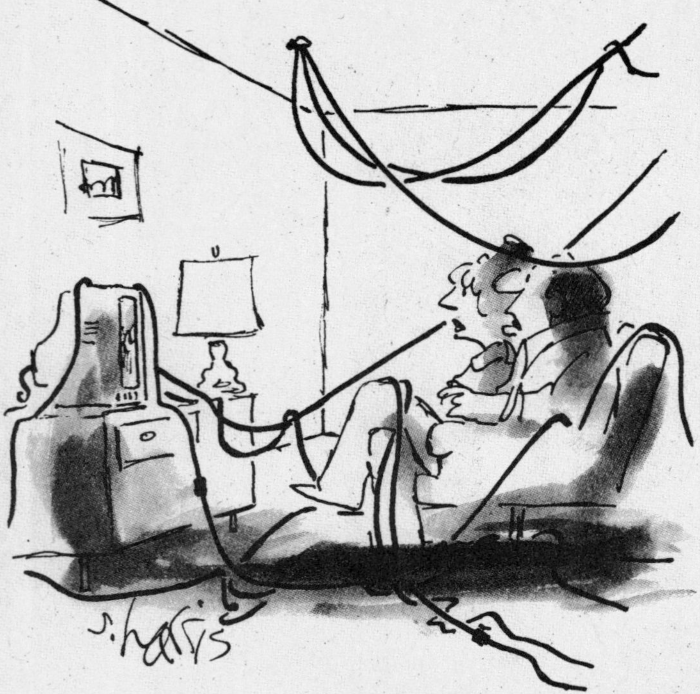

"Somehow I thought cable TV would be a lot simpler."

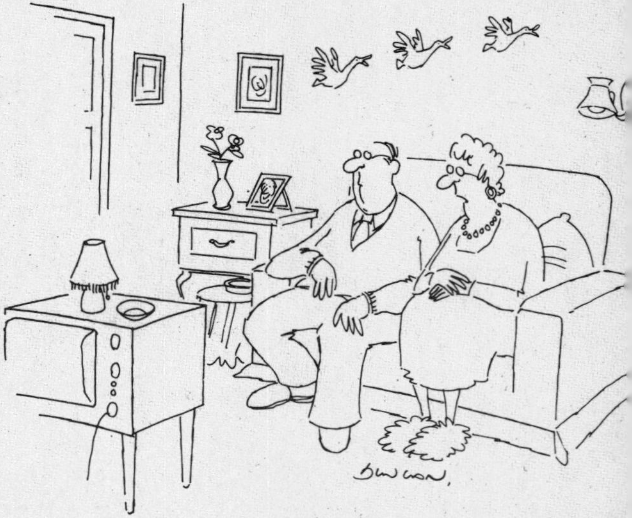

"I wonder what's on that we said we wouldn't watch."

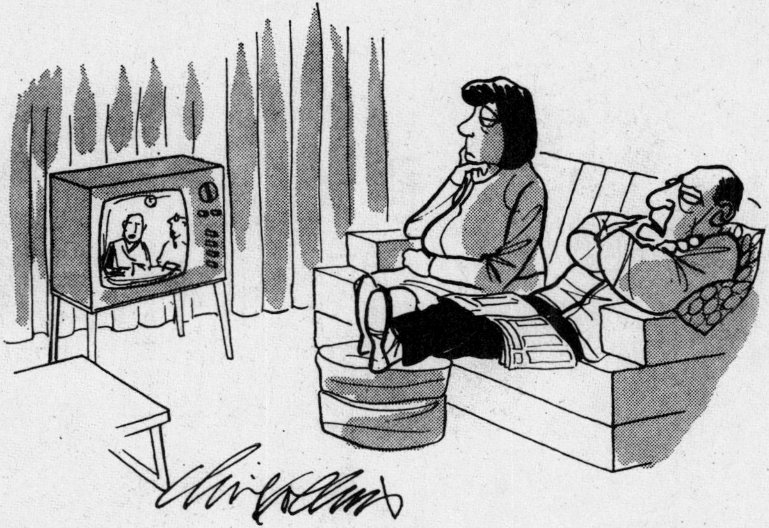

"It's marvellous when you come to think about it – thanks to satellites, most of Europe is being bored stiff by this programme . . ."

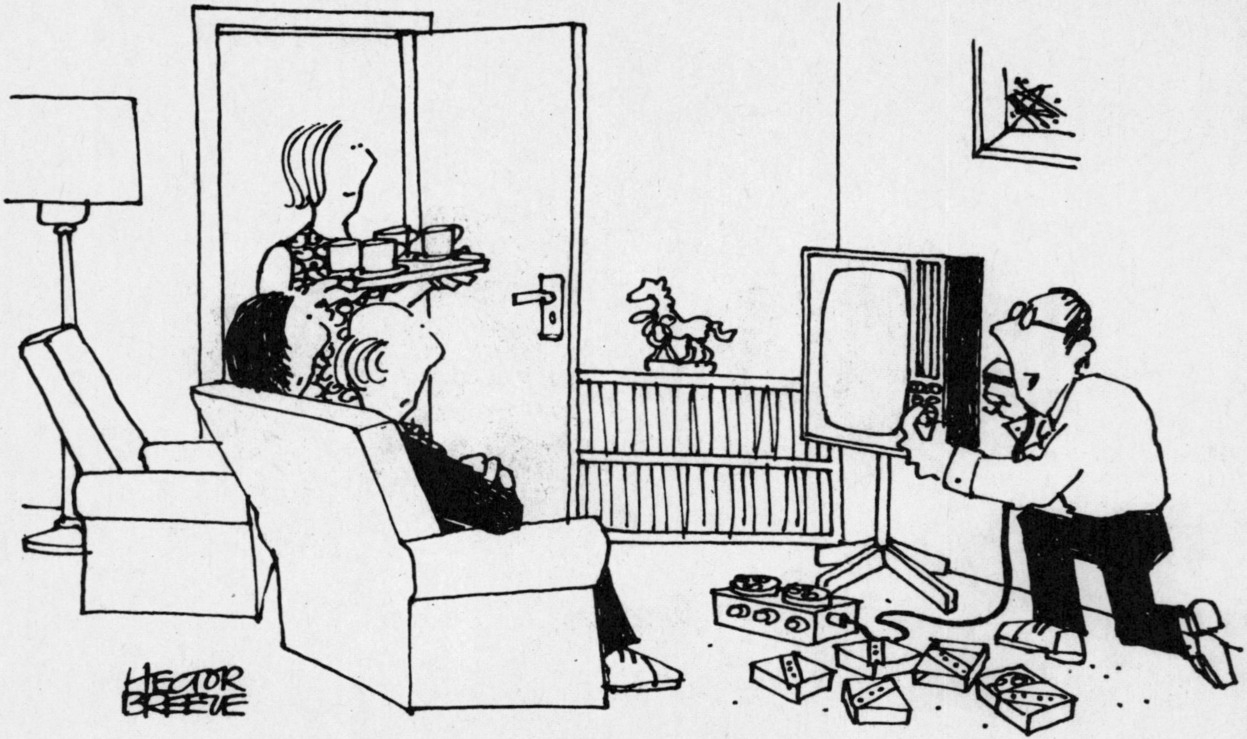

"Fortunately we managed to get on cassette some of the more interesting television we saw during our holiday."

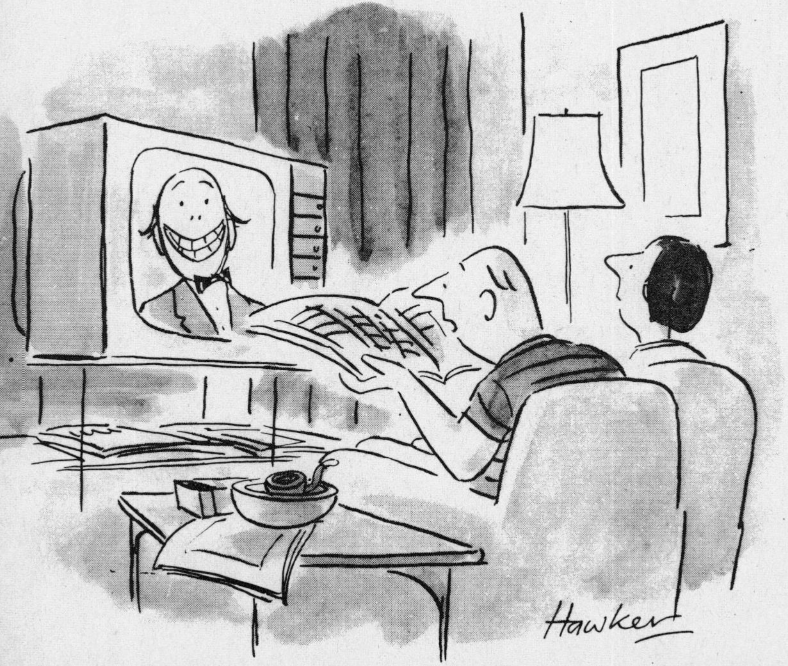

"Apparently he embarrassed royalty."

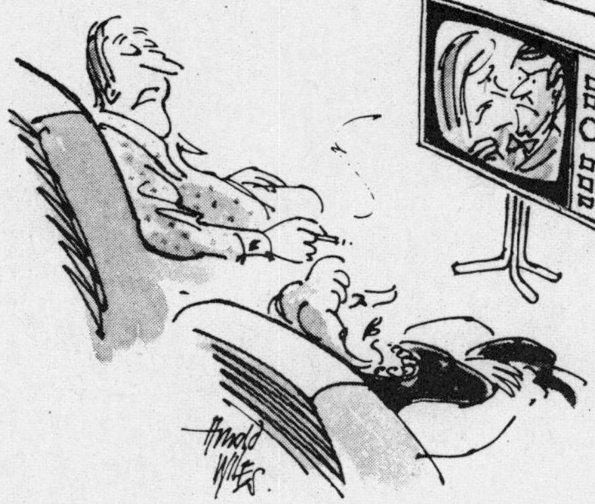

"Is this a bit part from when he was unknown or a guest appearance from when he was in the big-time?"

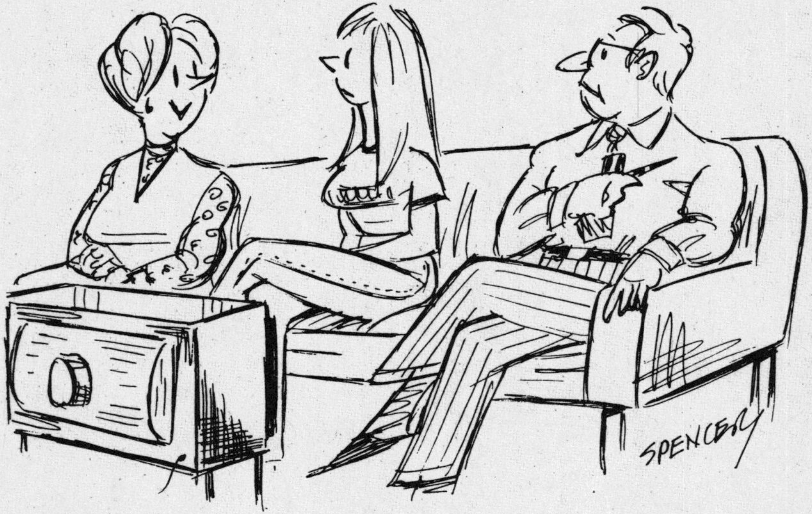

"It was at this point in the cinema that I felt a hand on my knee and that's how I met your father!"

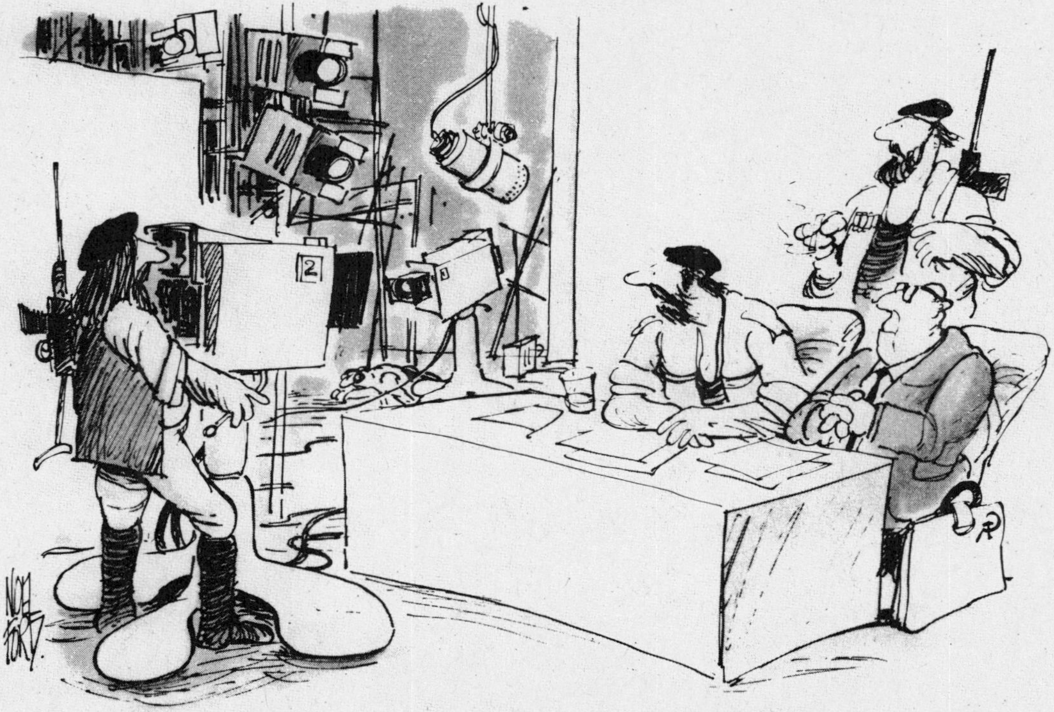

"More on the People's Revolution in a moment – first, a word from our sponsor. ."

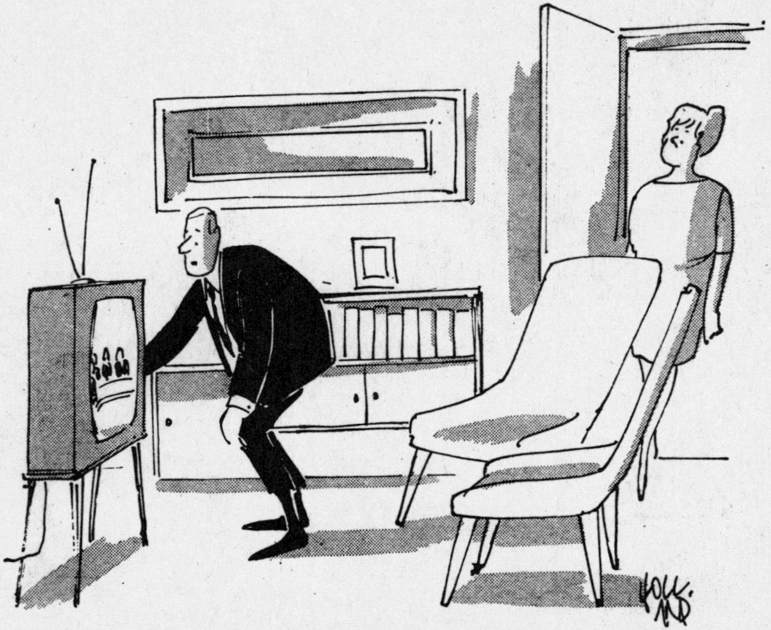

"There's a sociologist, a teenager, a psychiatrist and a humanist – it must be a religious programme."

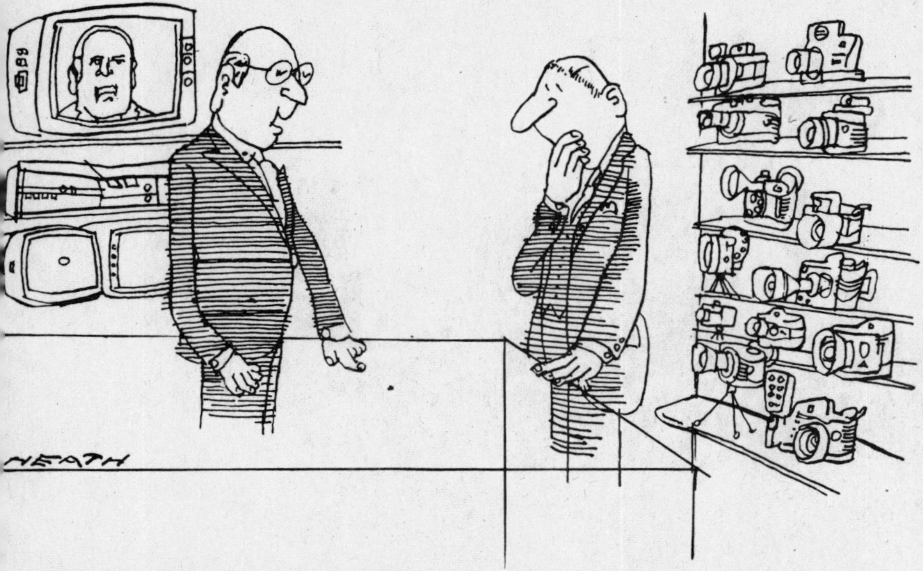

"It's the latest video-cassette recorder from Japan – all you do is add water."

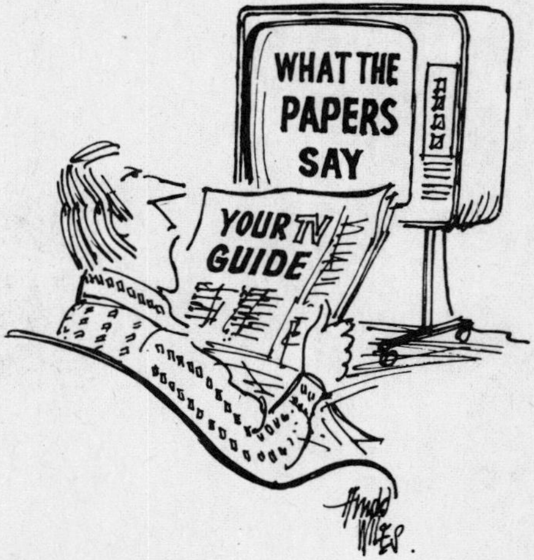

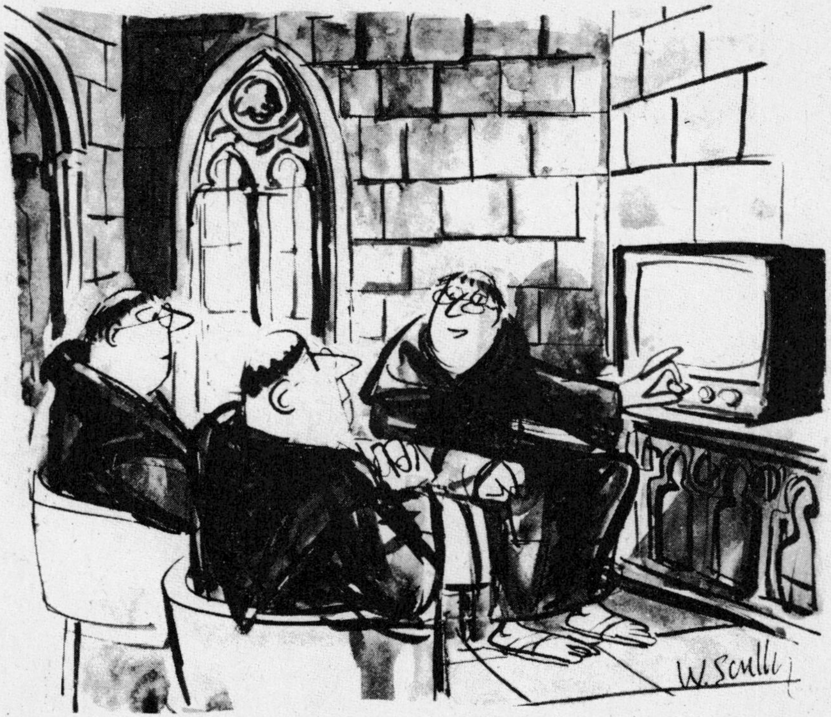

"Anyone for the Money Programme?"

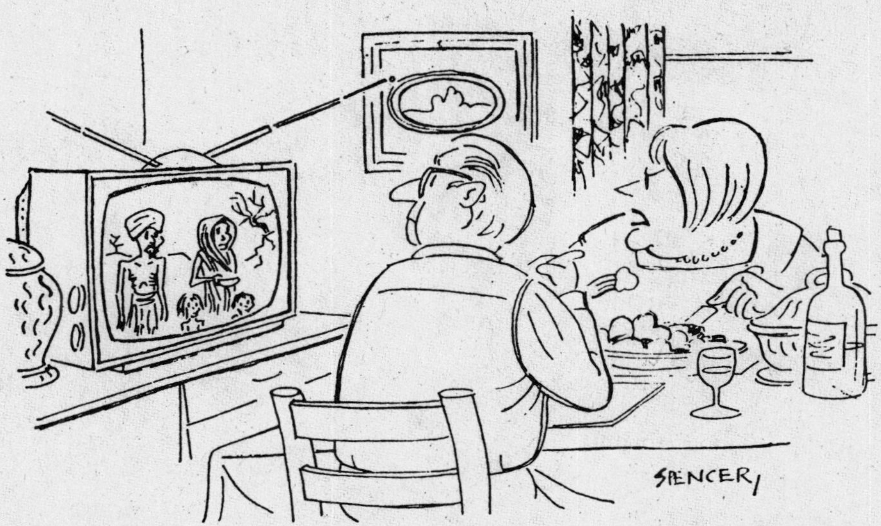

"Well, **really** – famine pictures at mealtimes!"

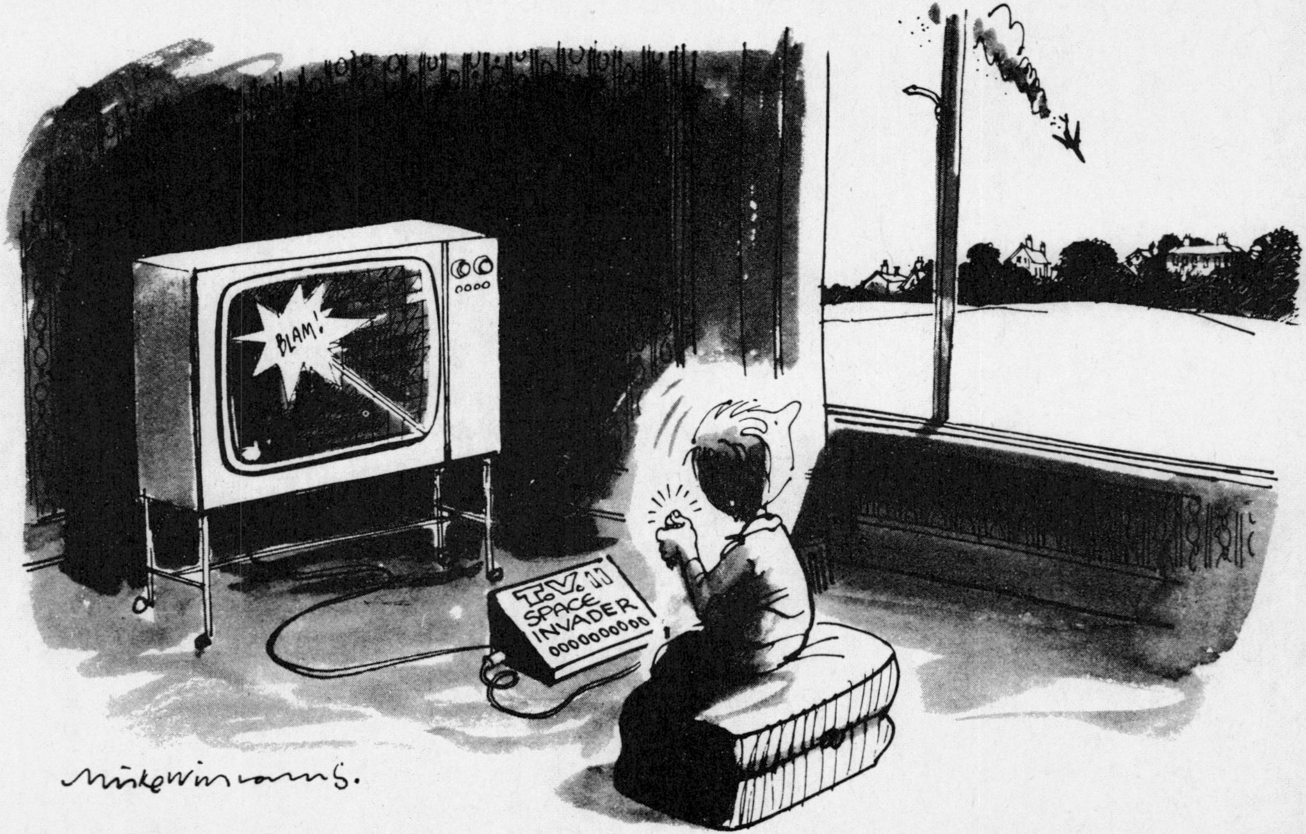
BLAM!
SPACE
INVADER

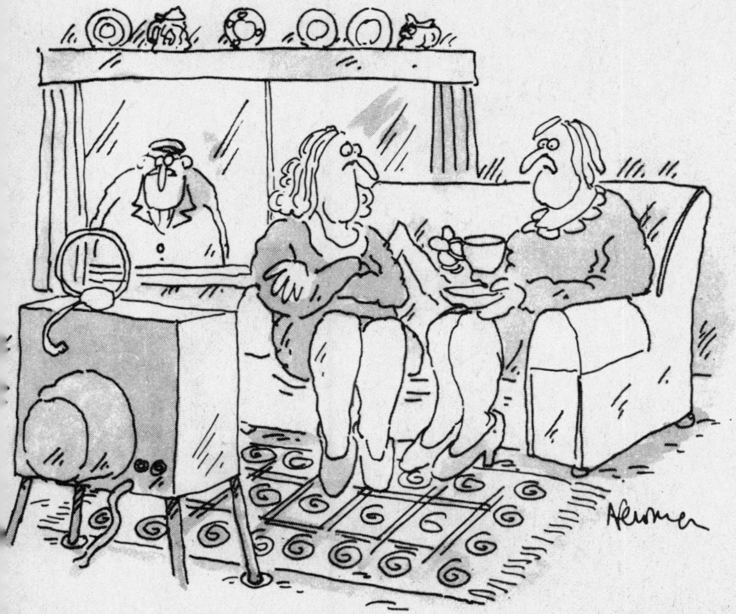

"He still hasn't got used to having a television . . ."

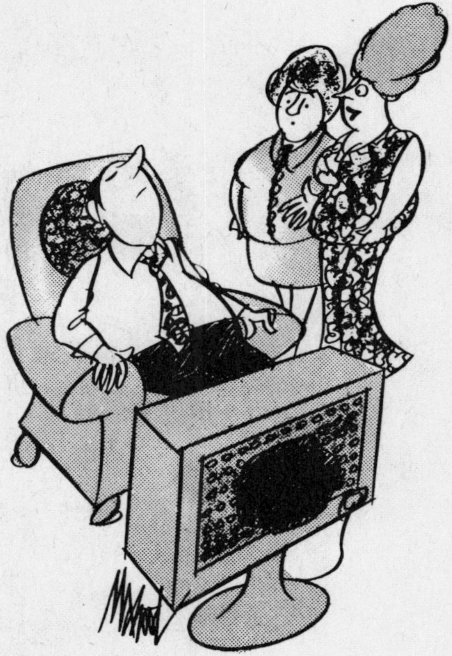

"Henry has begun serious training for an autumn election!"

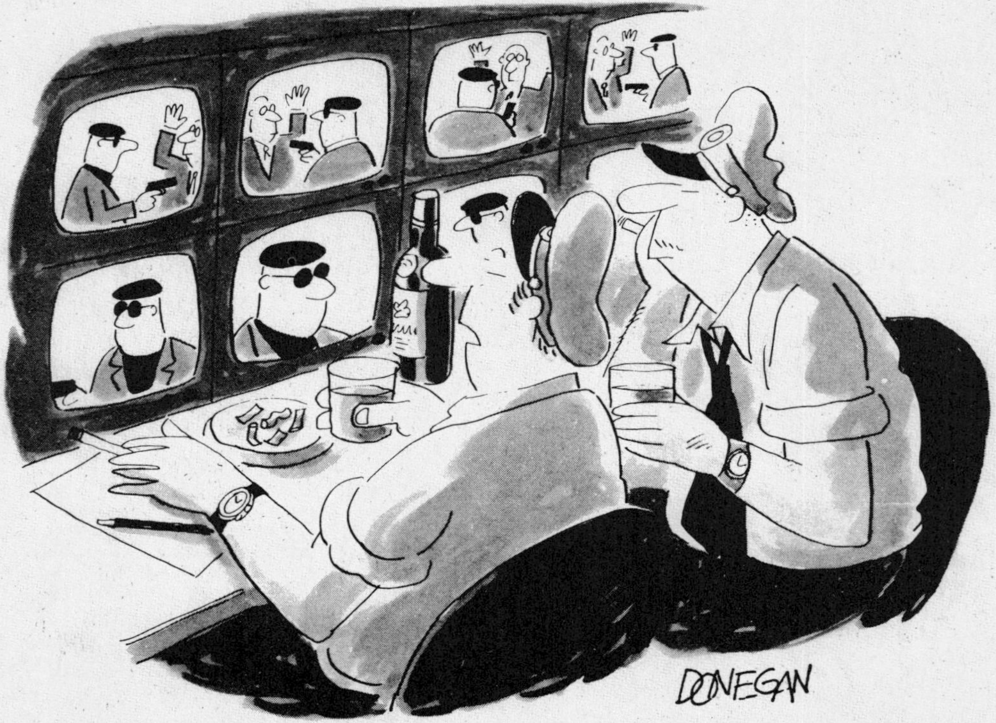

"No, can't be Ernie, he's still inside. Chas? Could be Chas or Maurice. I reckon it's Maurice. Remember Maurice, Elsie's brother. . .?"

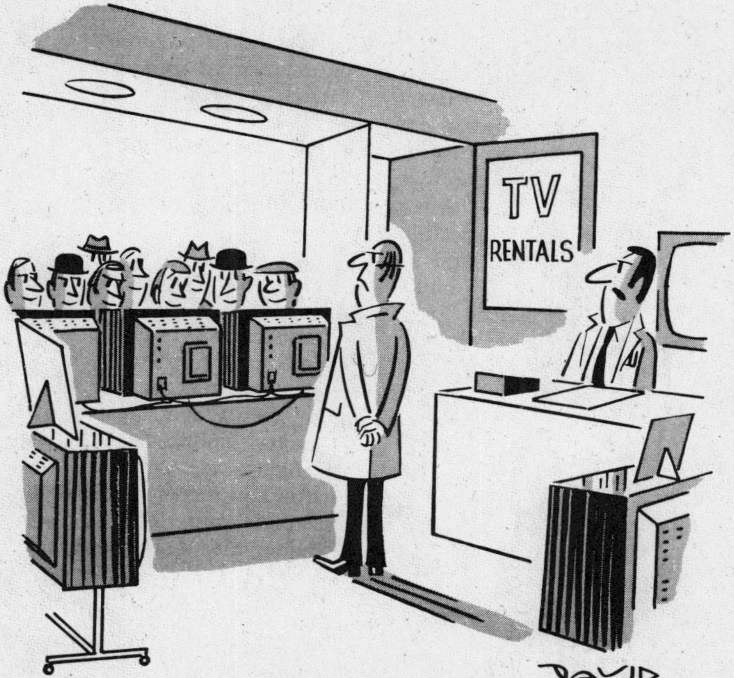

"World Cup, Test, Wimbledon – you'd think at least one of 'em would have the decency to pop a head in and say 'Thank you'."

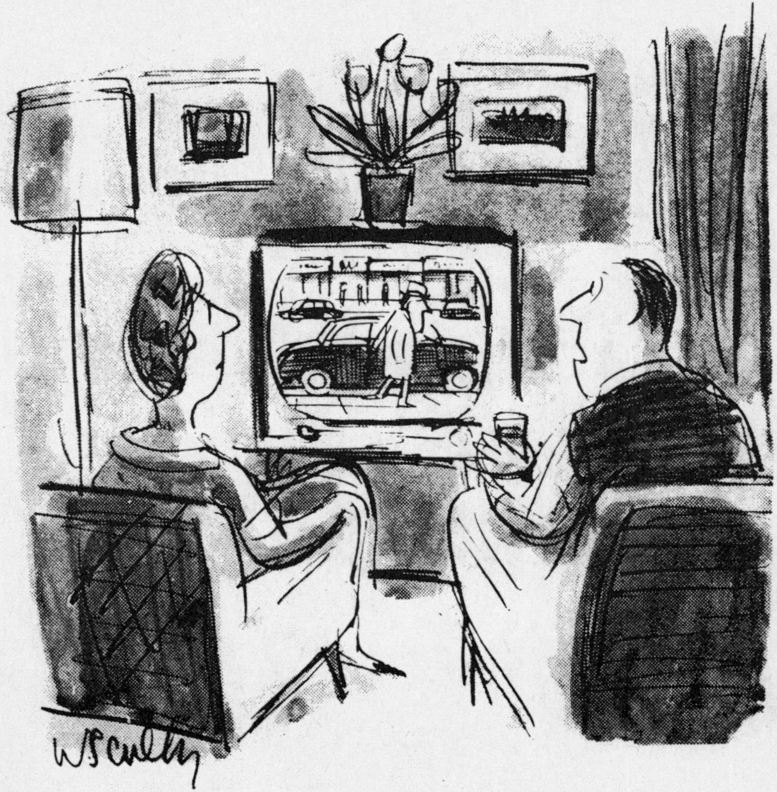

"God, how far fetched! It's only in The Wednesday Play that people can park as easily as that."

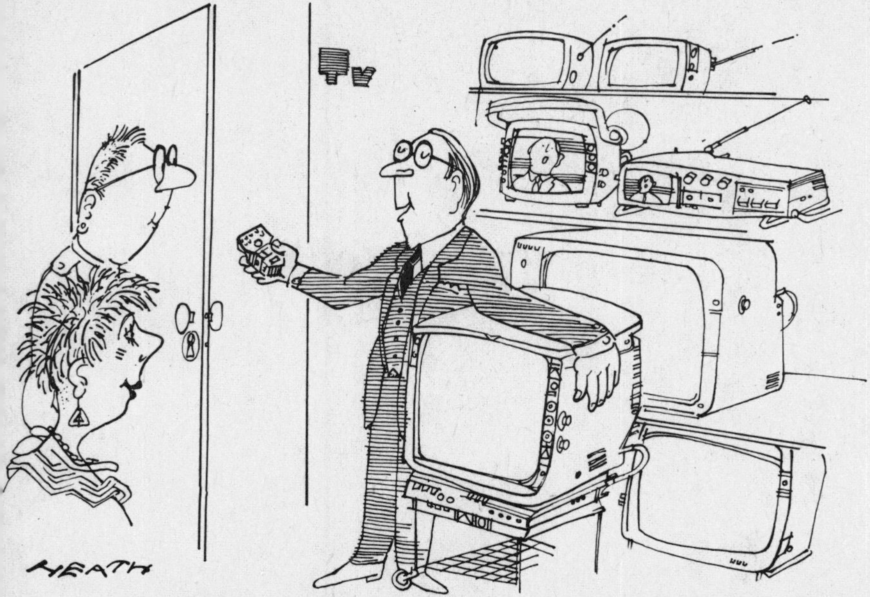

"And if there's a programme on you don't like, you just point this at the door which will open and you can walk out."

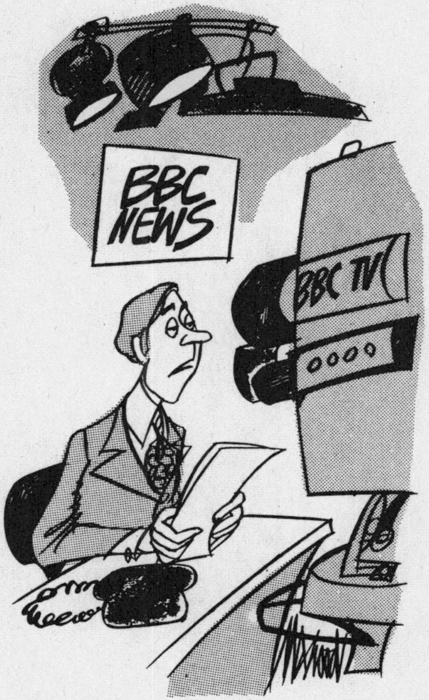

"Tonight we have three holding up to ransoms, ten ultimatums, six deadlocks, four hardening of attitudes, seven confrontations, three round-the-clock talks and no cooling-offs . . ."

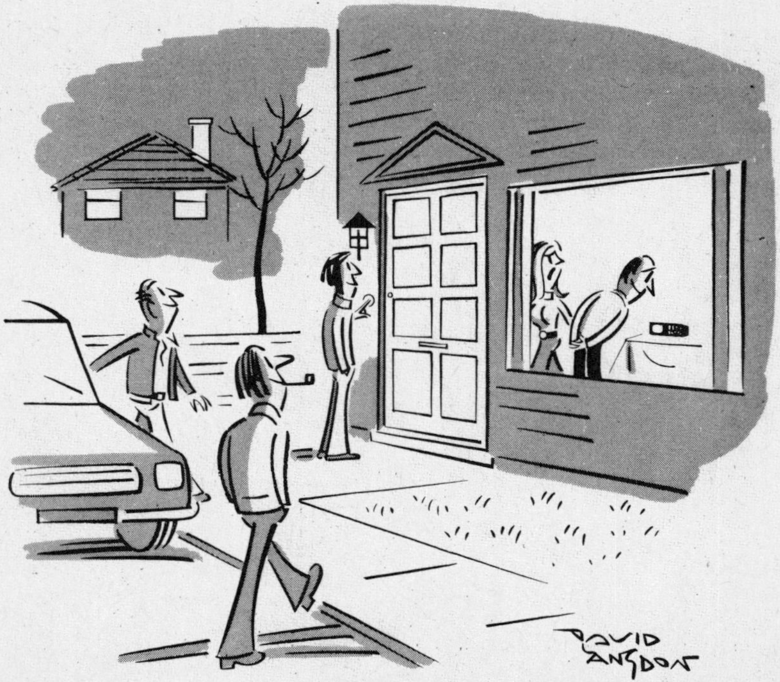

"Years ago it was Come round and see our twenty-six inch colour, now it's Come round and see our two inch black and white."

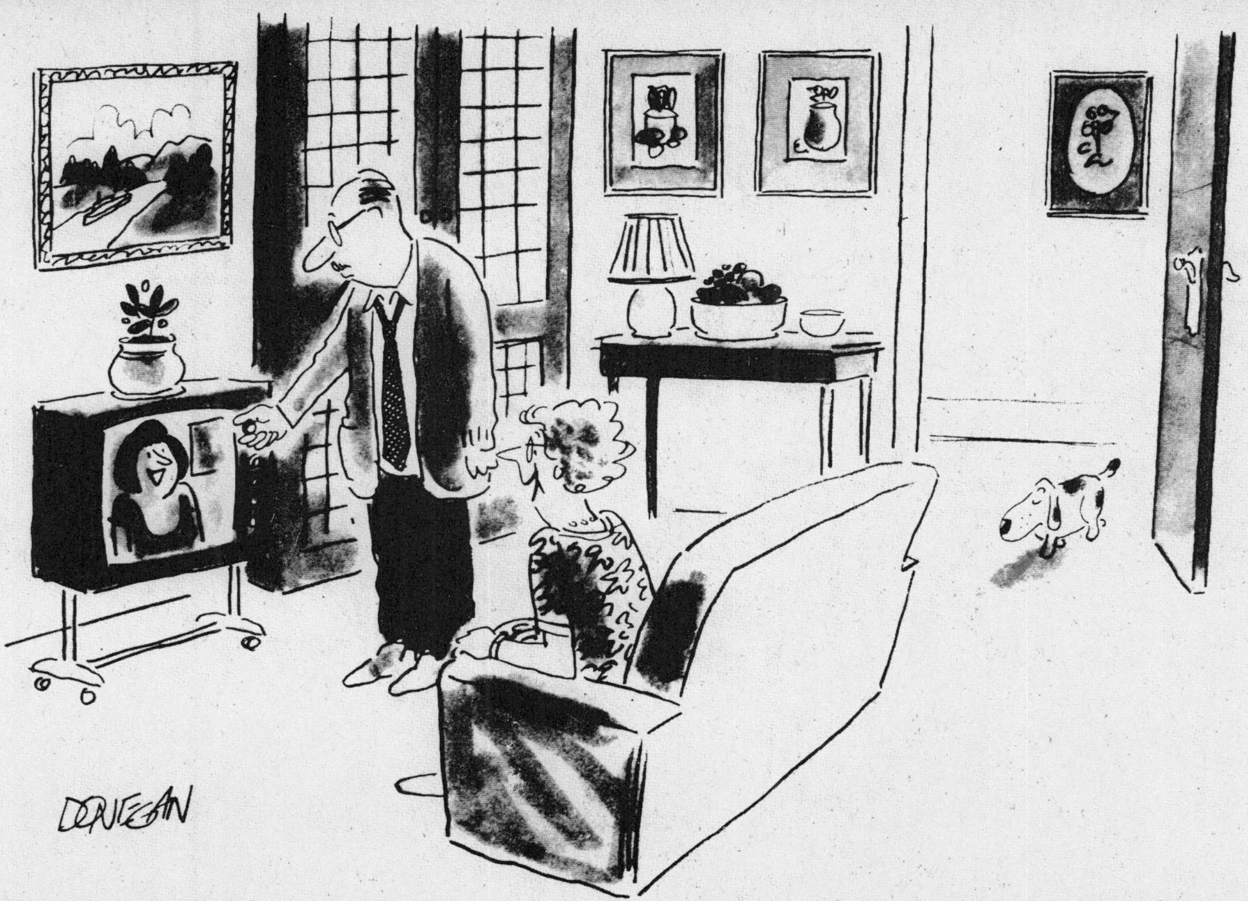

"More colour, more! He likes lots and lots of colour."

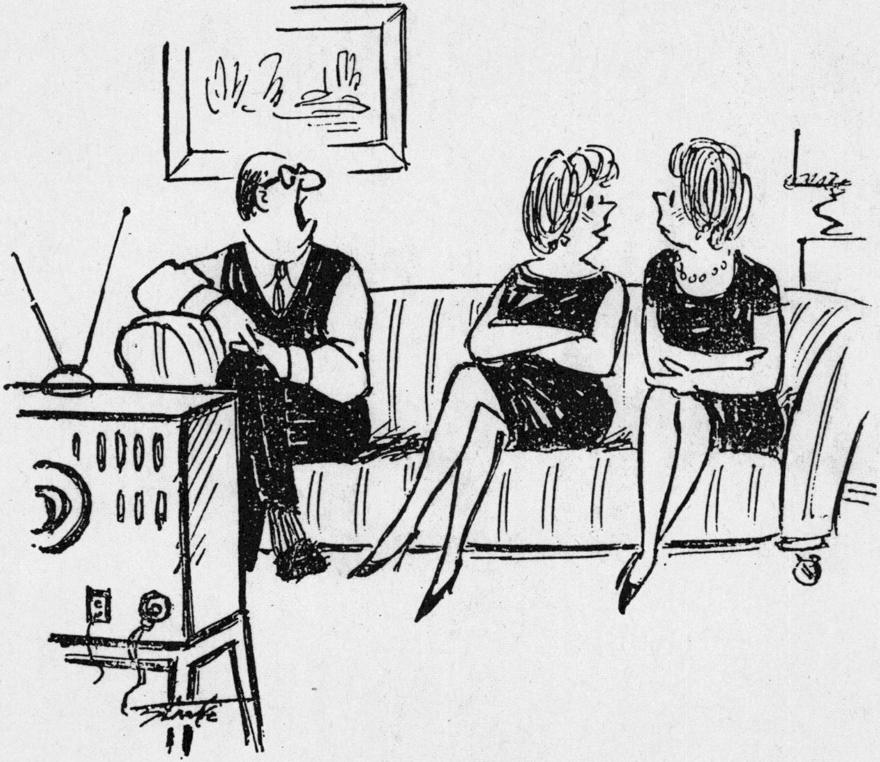

"Can't you two just accept that it **has** killed the art of conversation!"

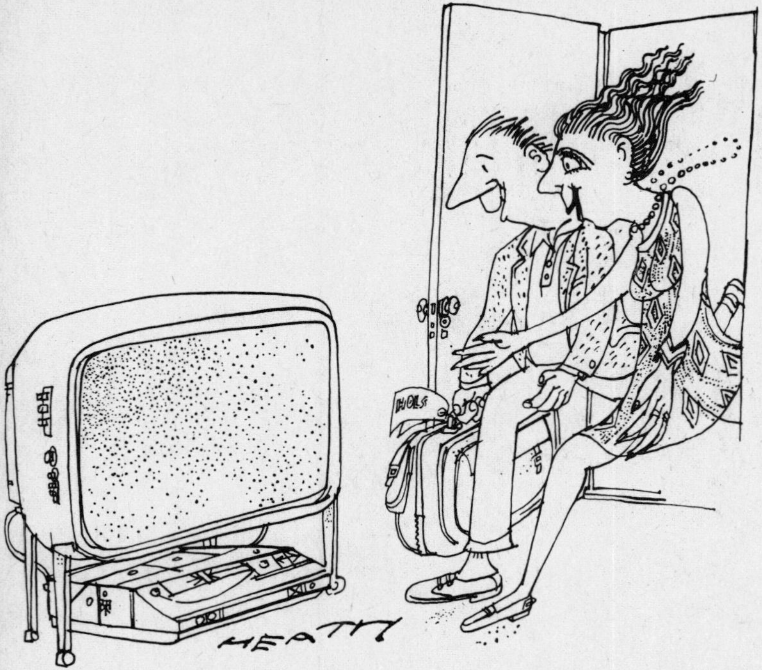

"We're home!"

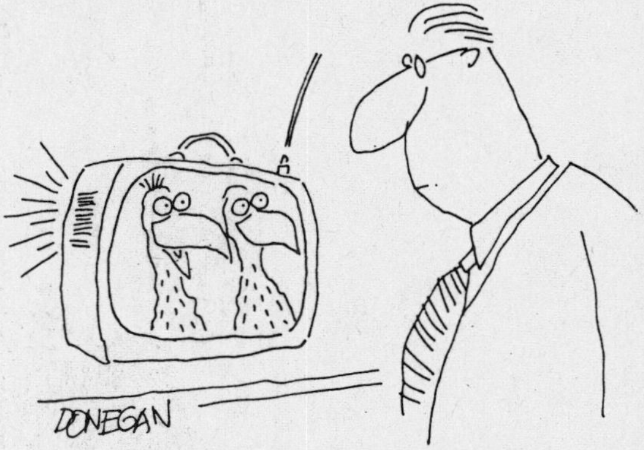

"For the moment we seem to be unable to return you to Richard Baker in the studio. In the meantime, no doubt you'd like to see our hitherto unseen courtship display again."

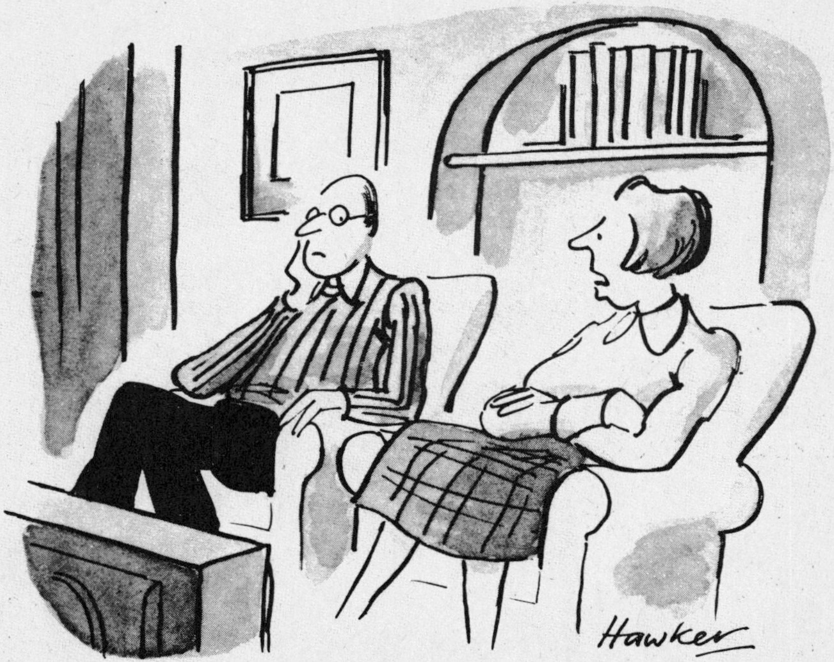

"Remember how we rushed home to watch this film when it was first shown on television?"

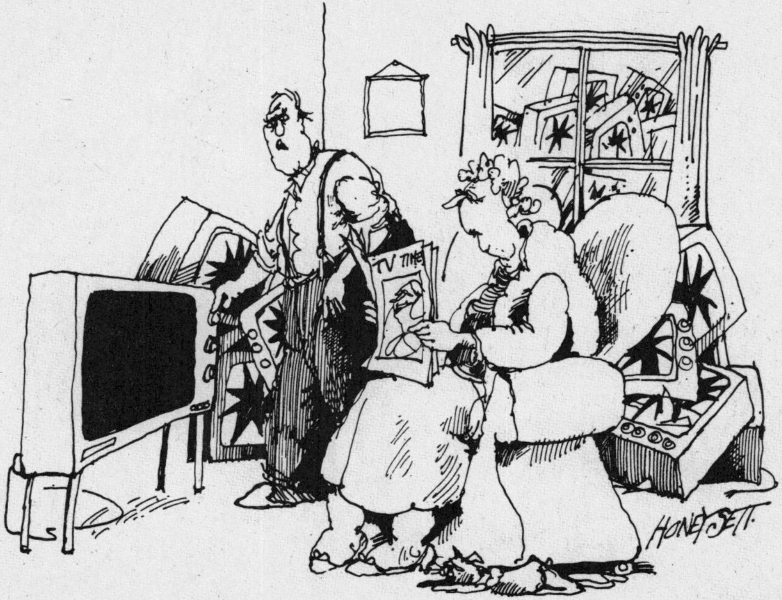

"Anything outrageous on tonight?"

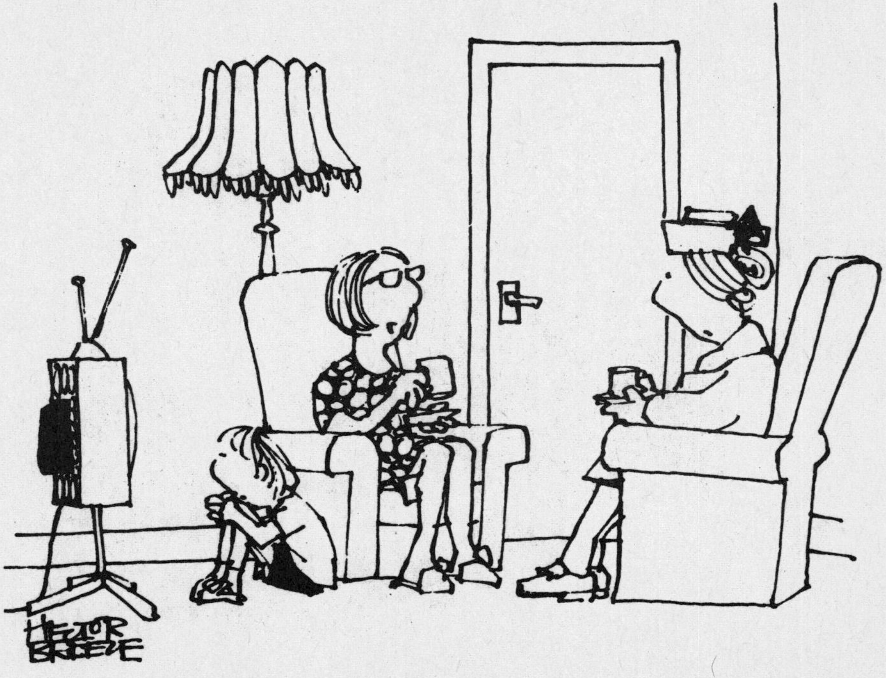

"The Educational Psychologist says he has a viewing age of twelve."

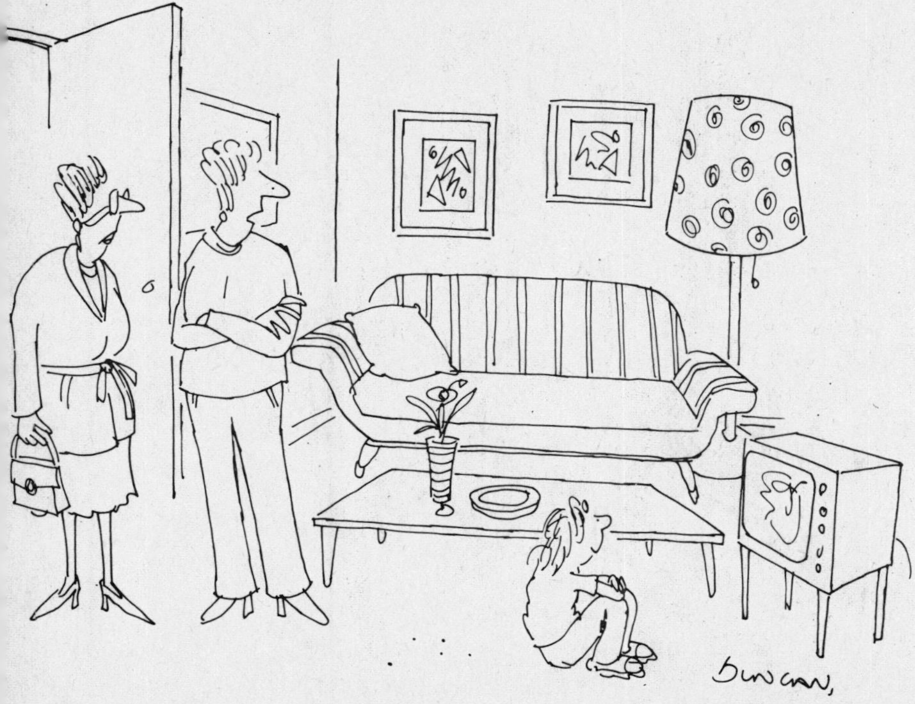

"I'm a little worried about her. Seven years old and still no interest in bargain offers."

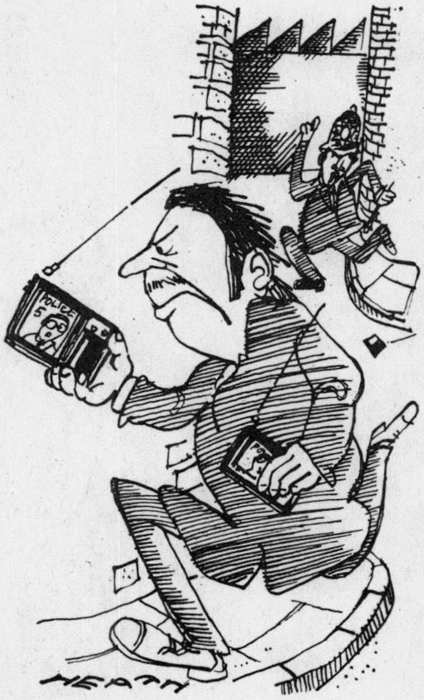

". . . So if some character comes up to you offering you a cheap pocket TV, ring the police."

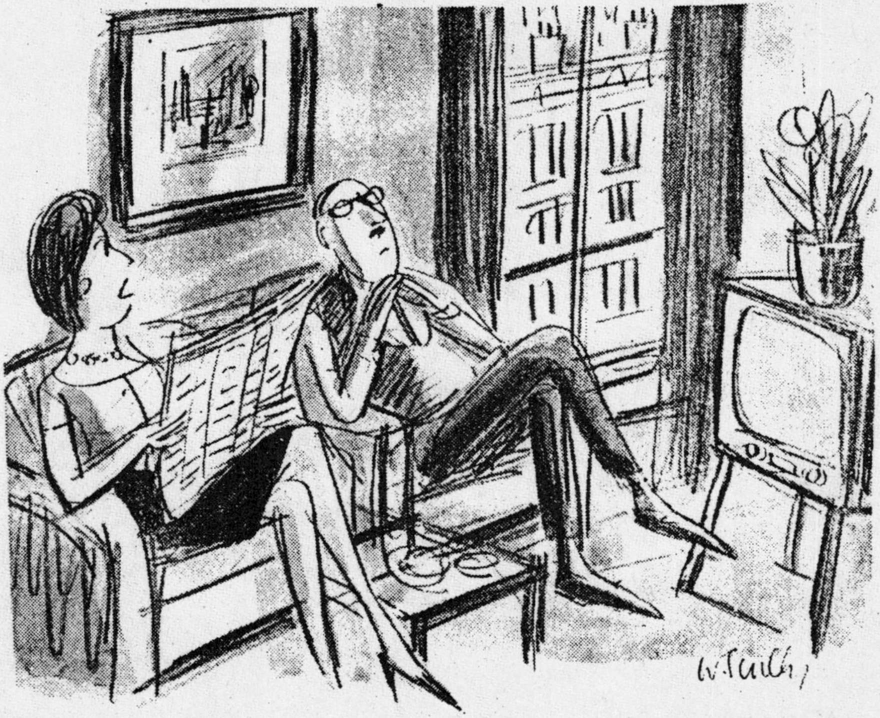

"For heaven's sake put the TV on, and stop sitting there thinking goodness knows what."

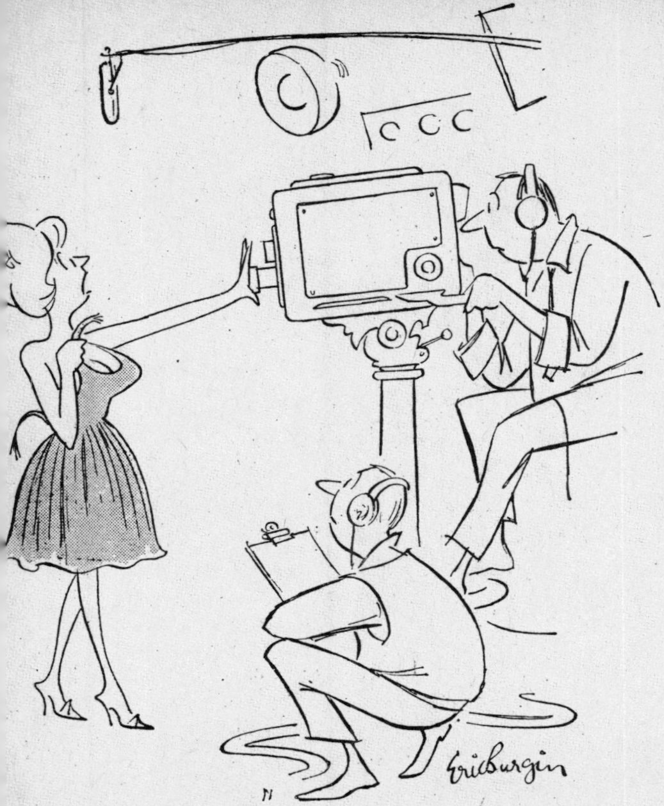

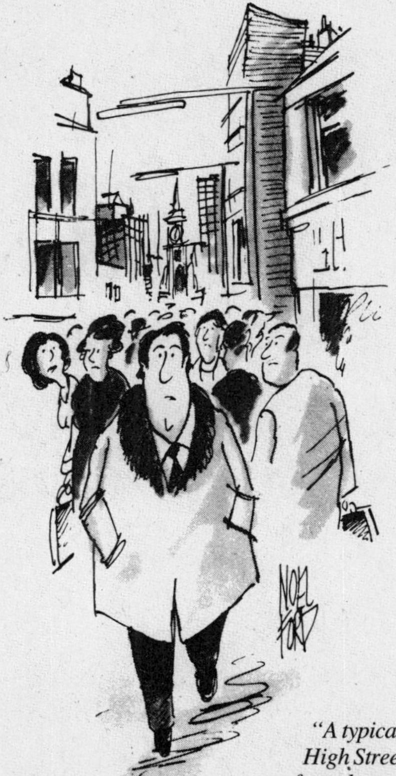

"A typical morning in Leicester High Street and, on the face of it, from the point of view of these early shoppers, just another TV reporter talking to a remote camera. Well, that's not quite true – the fact is, I'm off my head."

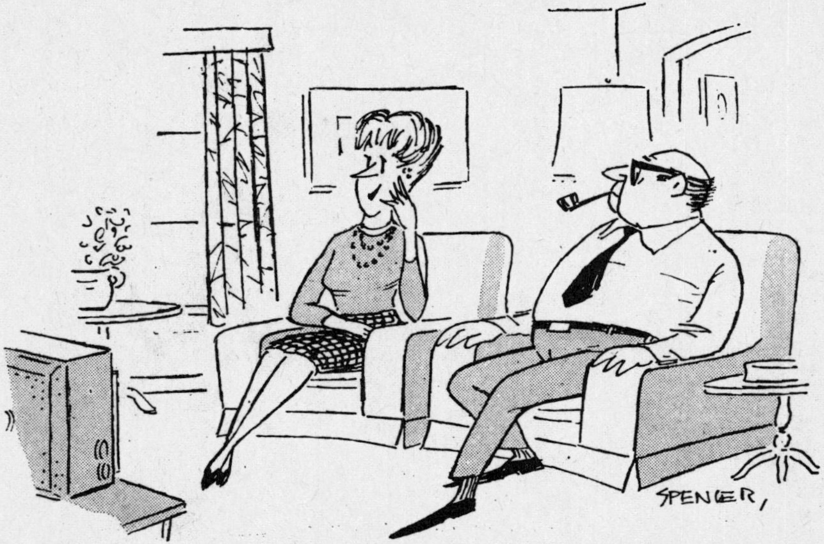

"Funny how the hero always grows lean and grey – never fat and bald."

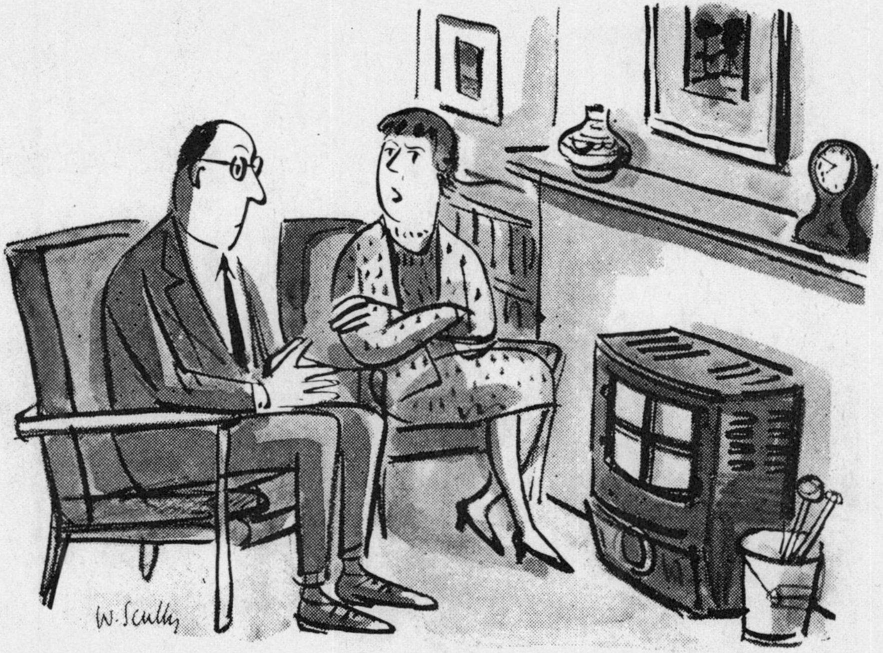

"You might get a brighter picture with the doors open!"

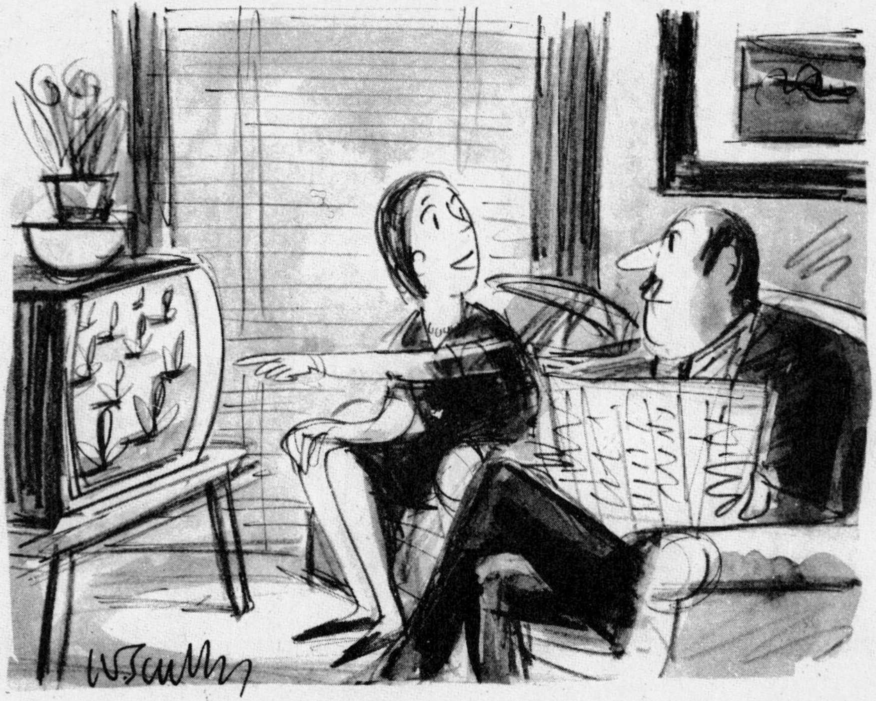

"Why, look! The first crocuses!"

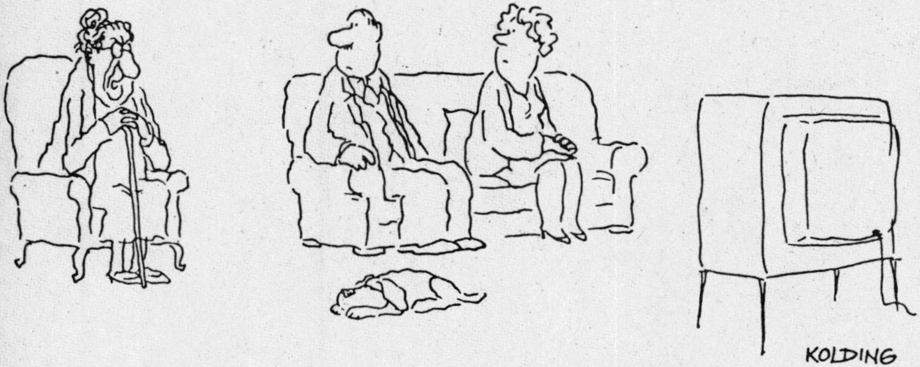

"Martha Bolton, mother of Nora, mother-in-law of Geoffrey, this is your life."

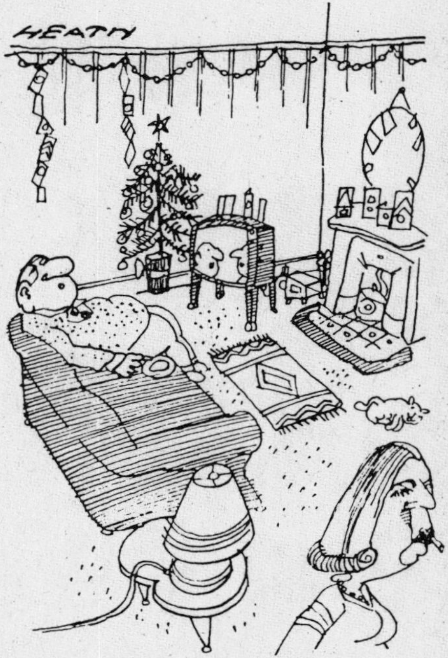

"Well, that's Christmas sorted out then – the first half of 'Gone with the Wind' here and the second half over at your mother's on Boxing Day."

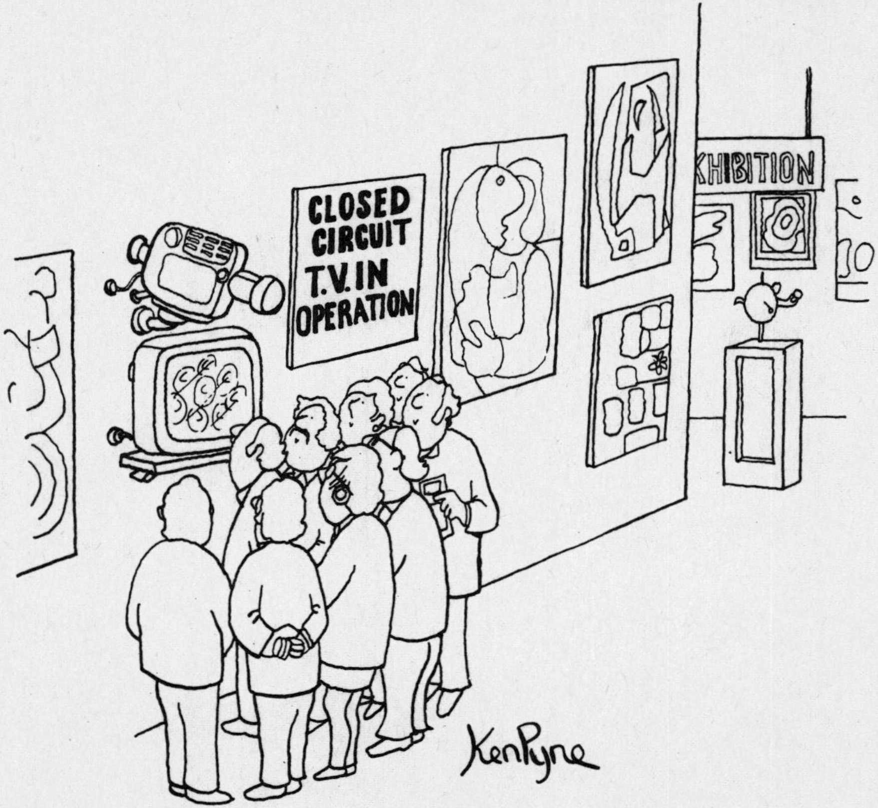
CLOSED
CIRCUIT
T.V. IN
OPERATION
XHIBITION
Ken Pyne

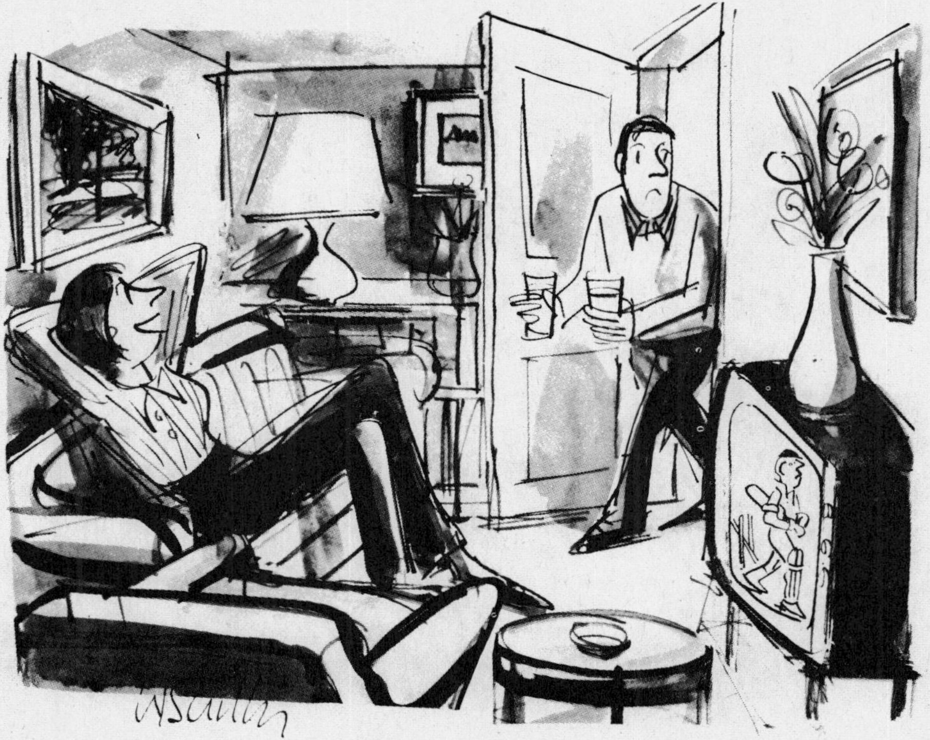

"Well, that's broken the long stand. You must go out for drinks more often."

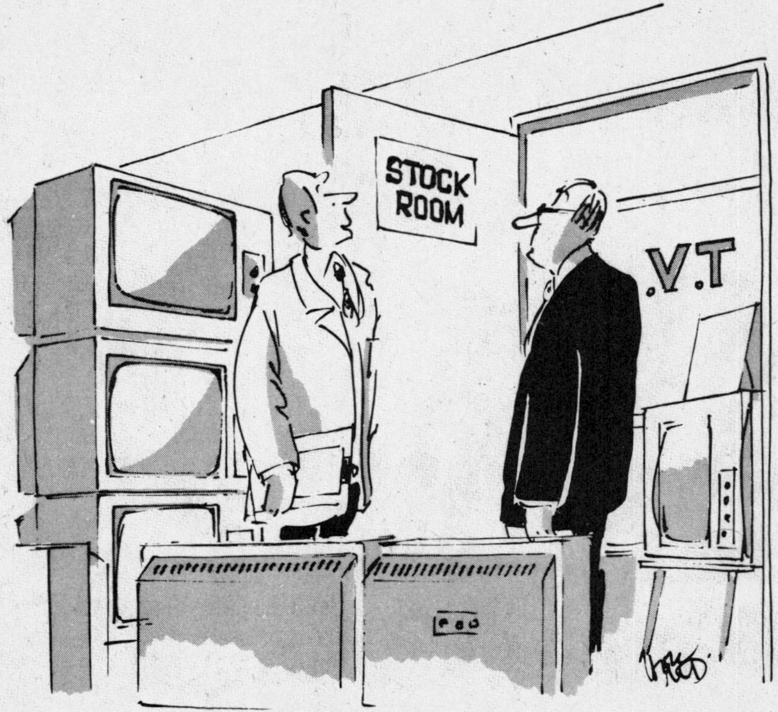

"We're preparing for the inevitable nostalgia boom in monochrome sets."

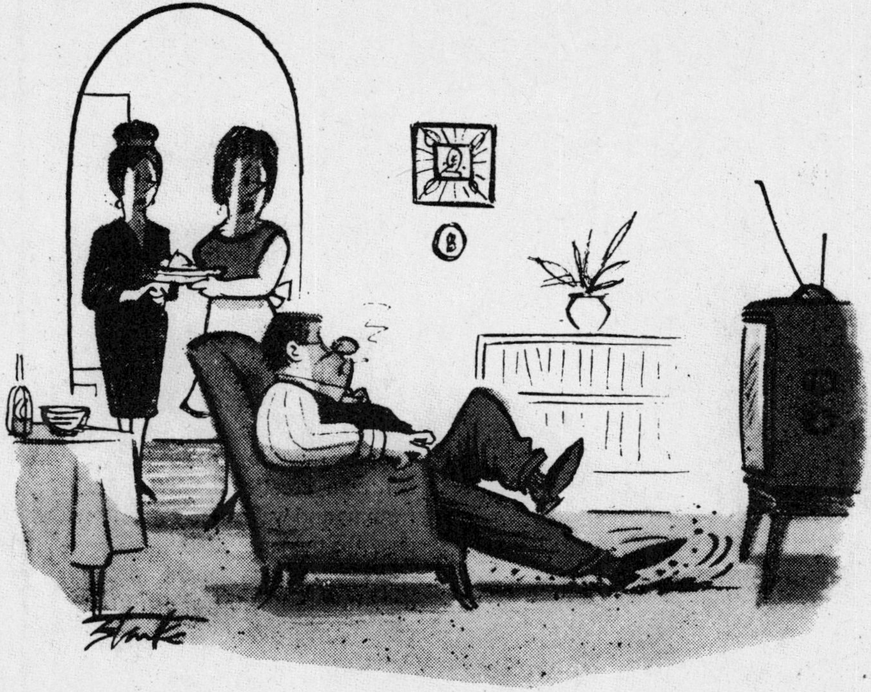

"I do wish they wouldn't tear up to the bends like that at Brands Hatch."

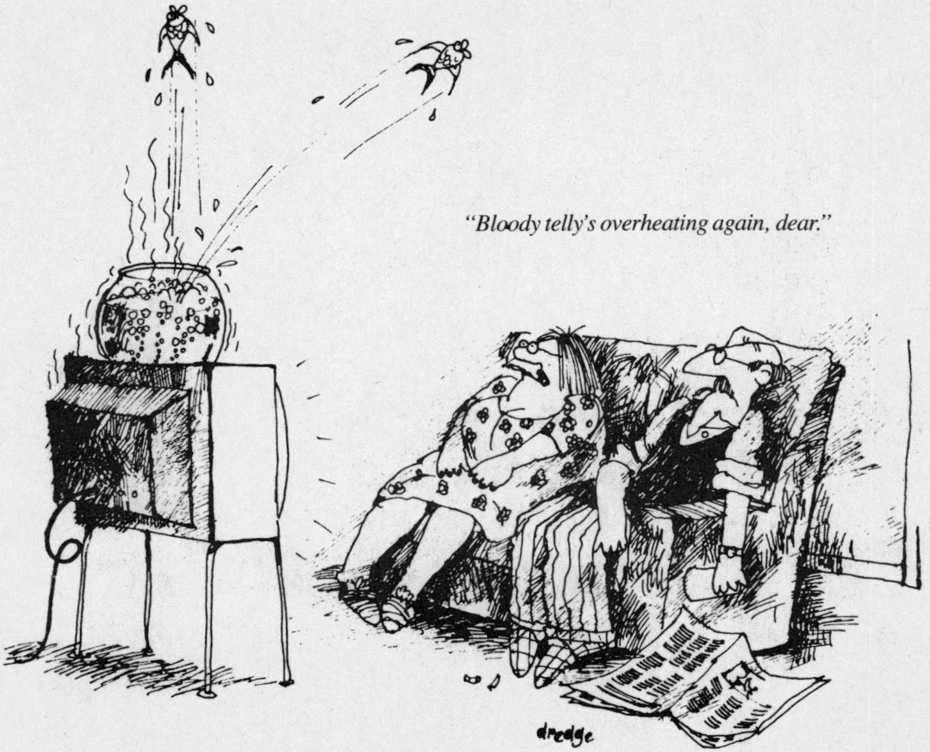

"Bloody telly's overheating again, dear."

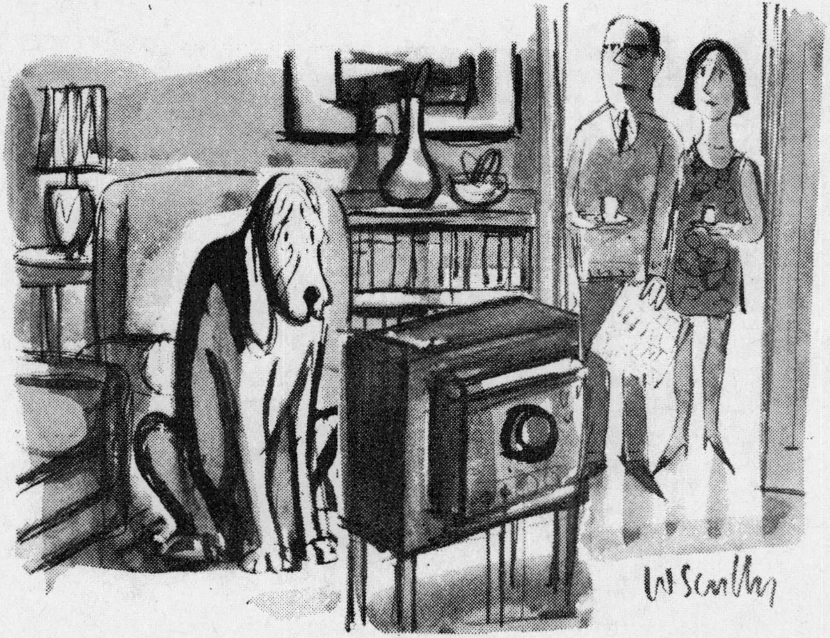

"I see Panorama's on."

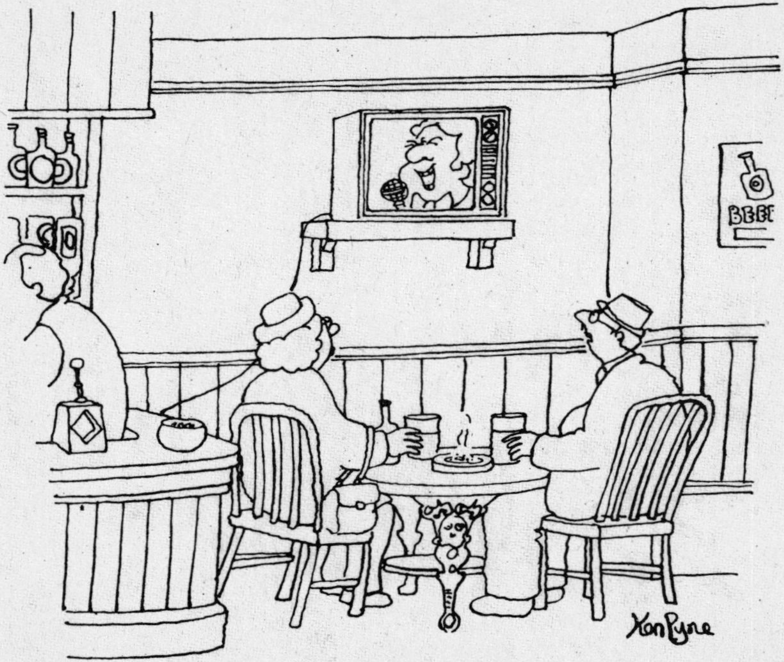

"It makes you wonder what kind of people stay at home just to watch this rubbish!"

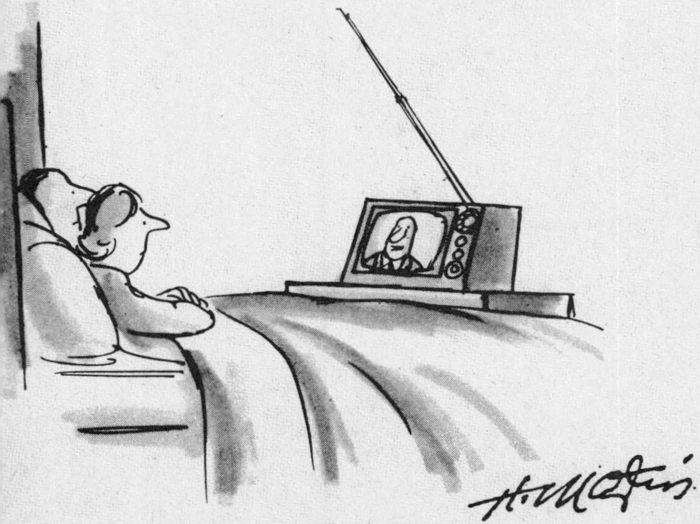

"Good evening. The following programme will probably offend all of you. The number to call in outrage is 246 8000. Thank you."

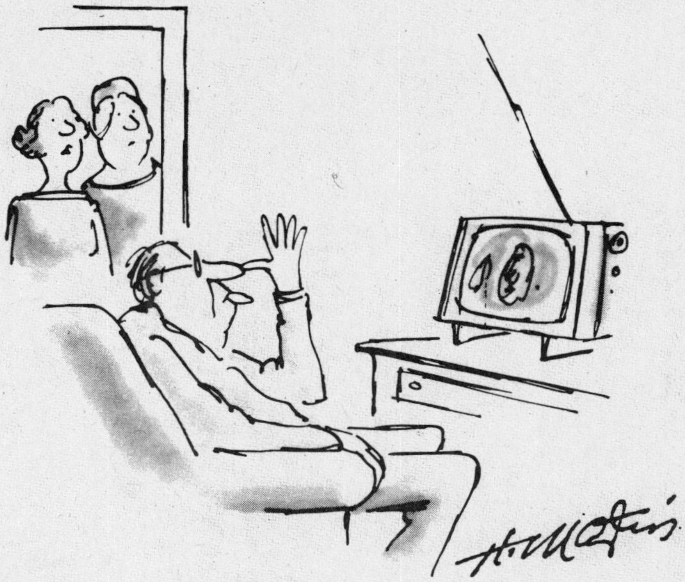

"Gordon never realised how much he really hated TV until after we bought a set."

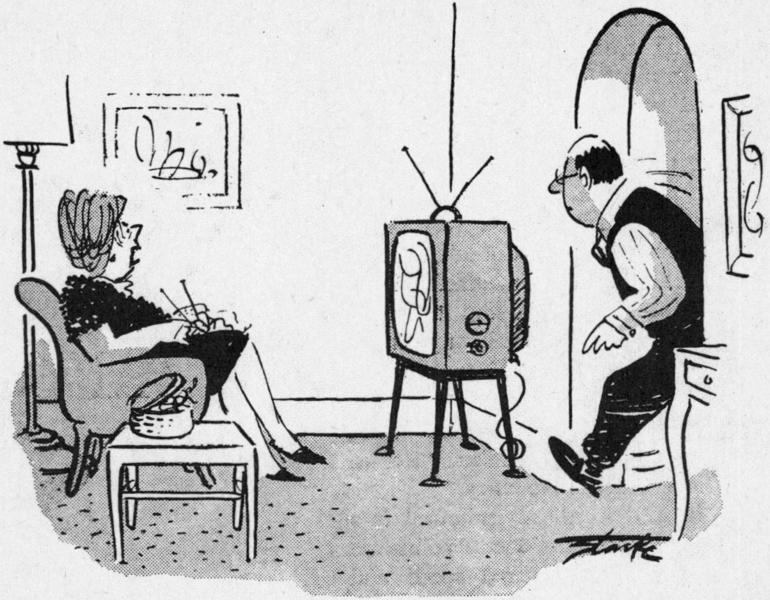

"Disgusting!"

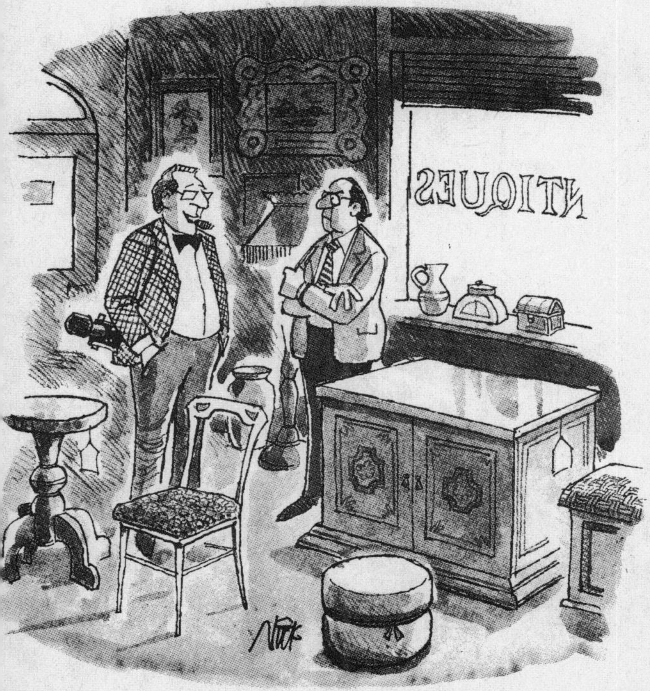

"Well, it sure looks like a television."

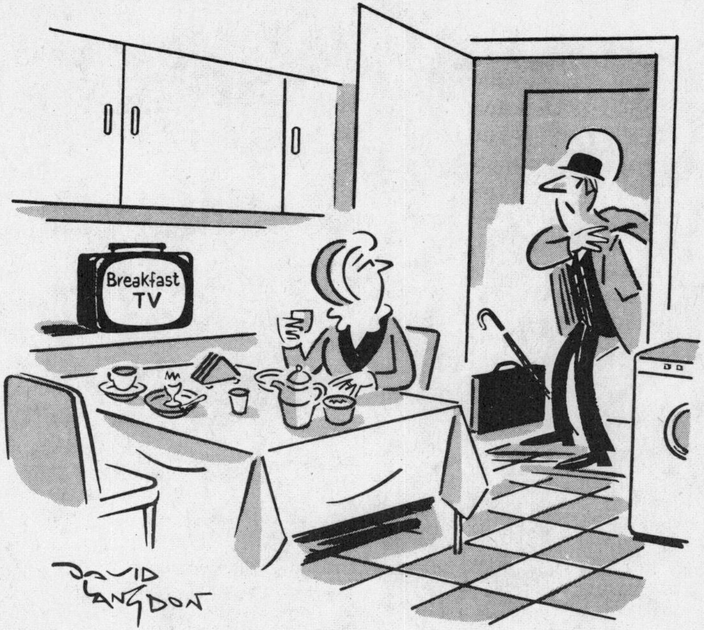

"Tape it and I'll watch it tonight."

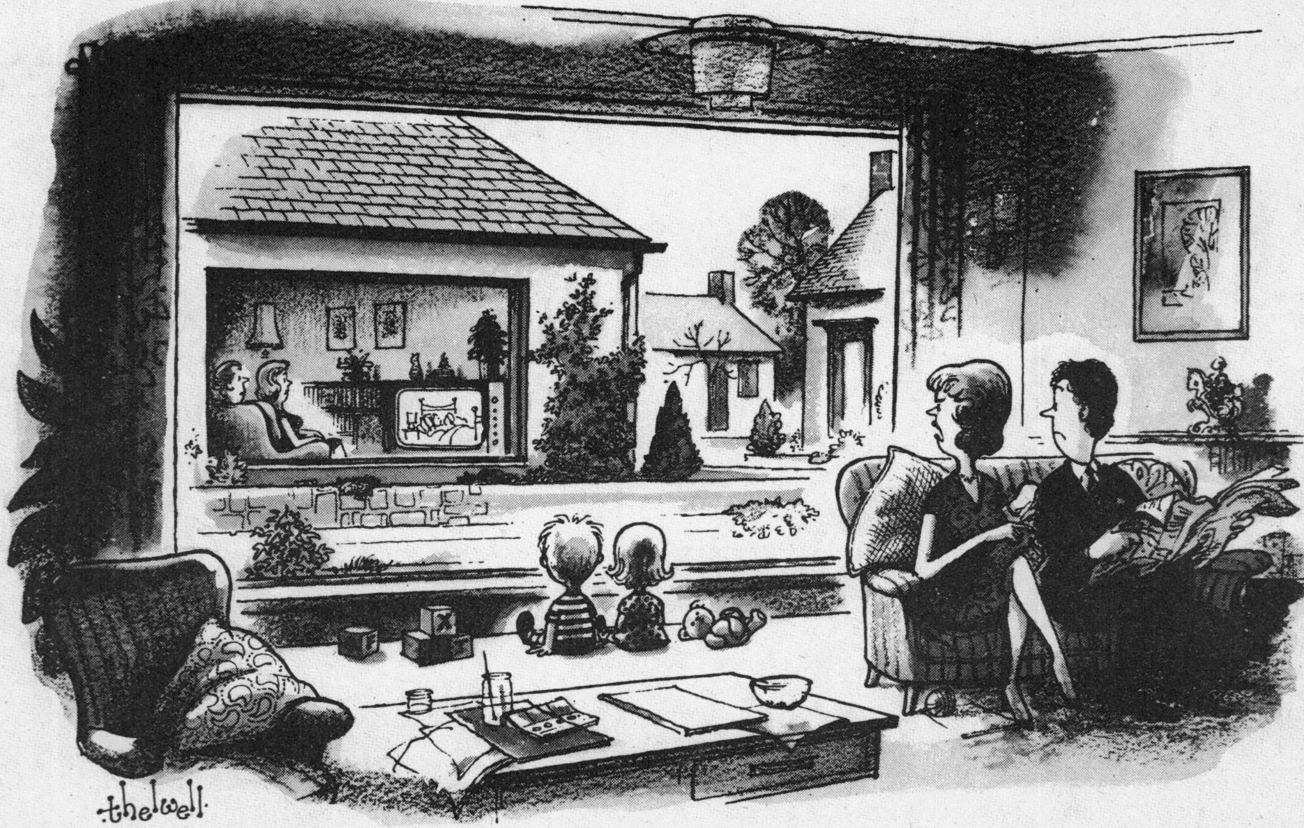

"I wish they wouldn't switch programmes like that on, before the children are in bed."

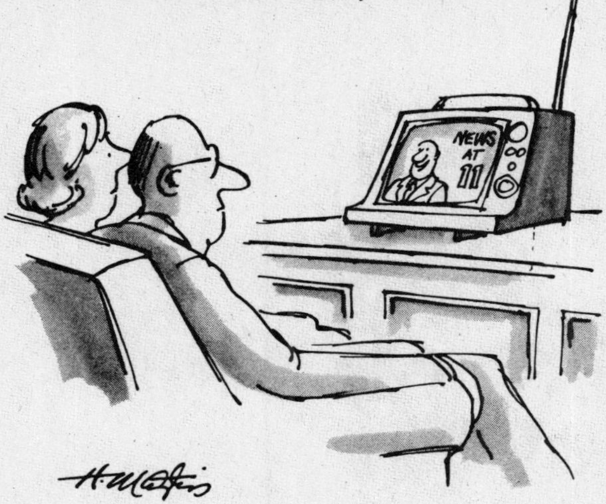

"I'd like to remind you all that the rapes, robberies and beatings you hear on 'News at Eleven' are not the same rapes, robberies and beatings you heard about on 'News at Five Forty-Five'."

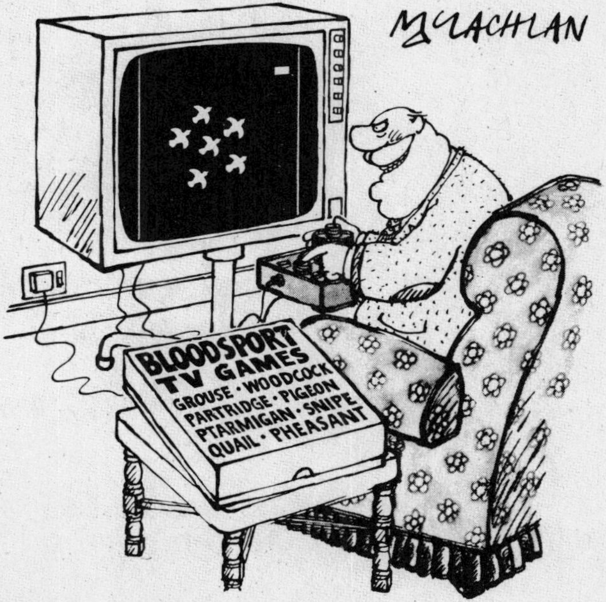

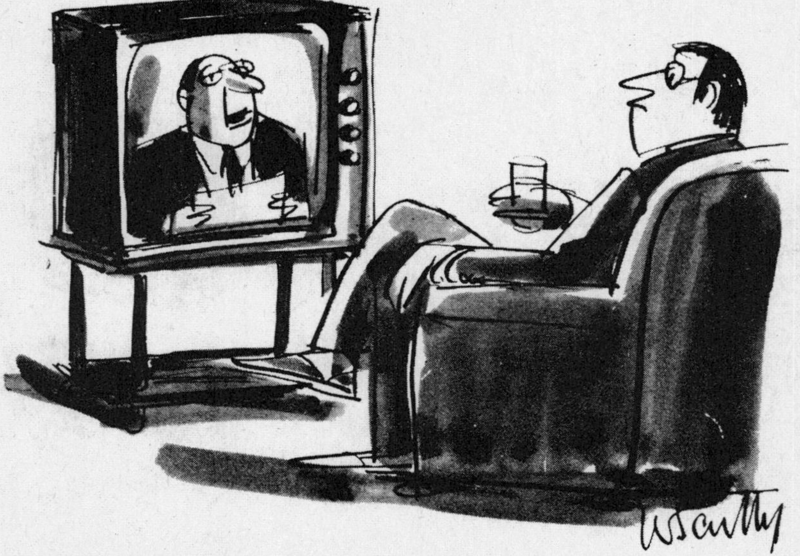

"The damage was slight and there were no casualties. The responsibility for the bomb was claimed by a moderate group."

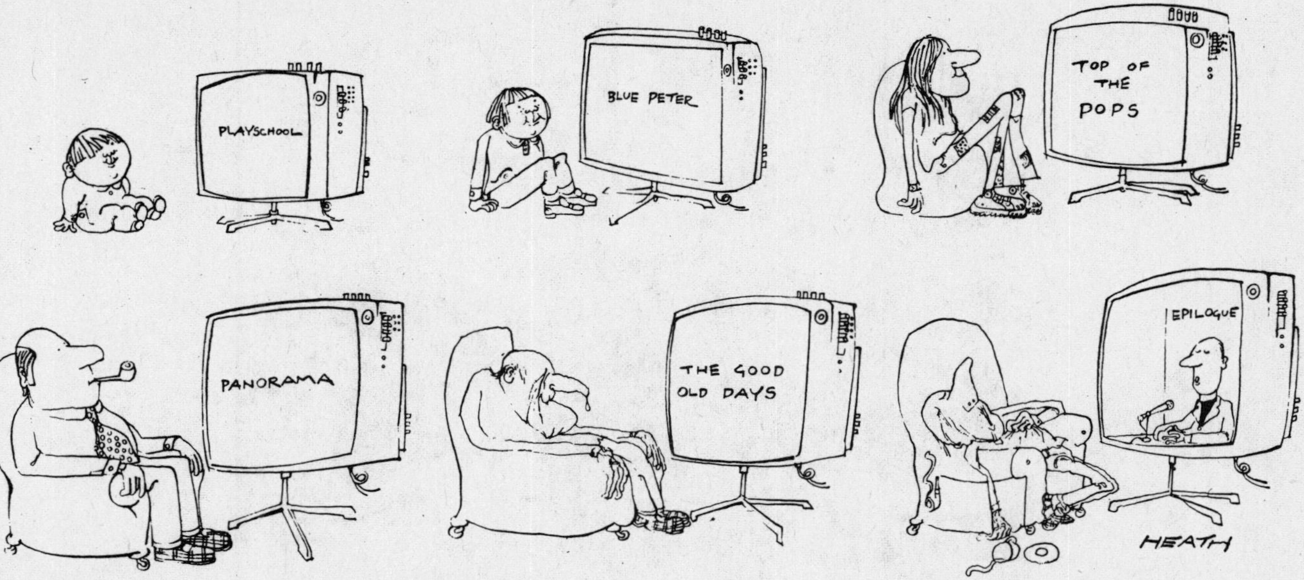
PLAYSCHOOL
BLUE PETER
TOP OF THE POPS
PANORAMA
THE GOOD OLD DAYS
EPILOGUE
HEATH

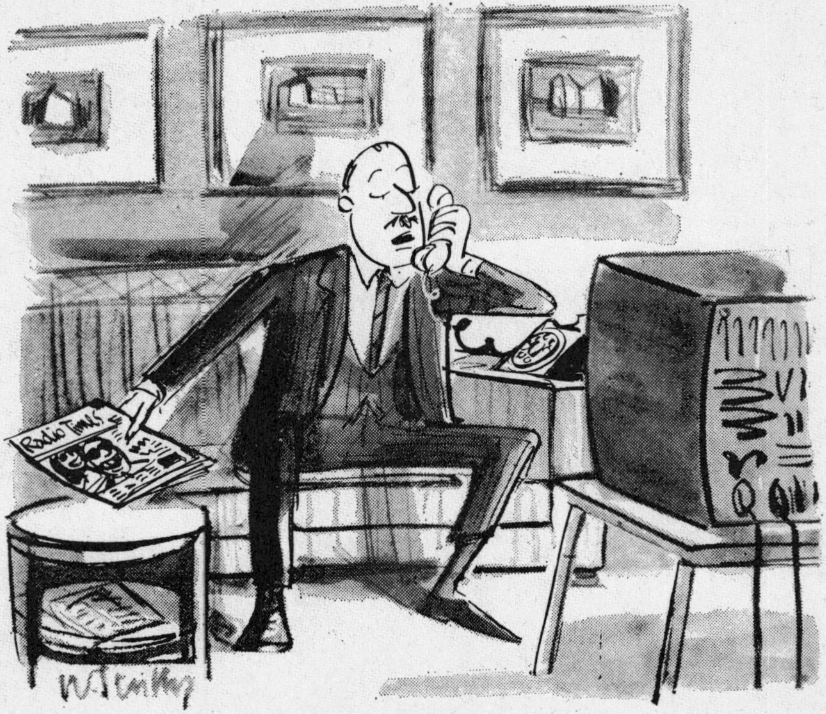

"Just a moment – I'll take a peep at our engagement book."

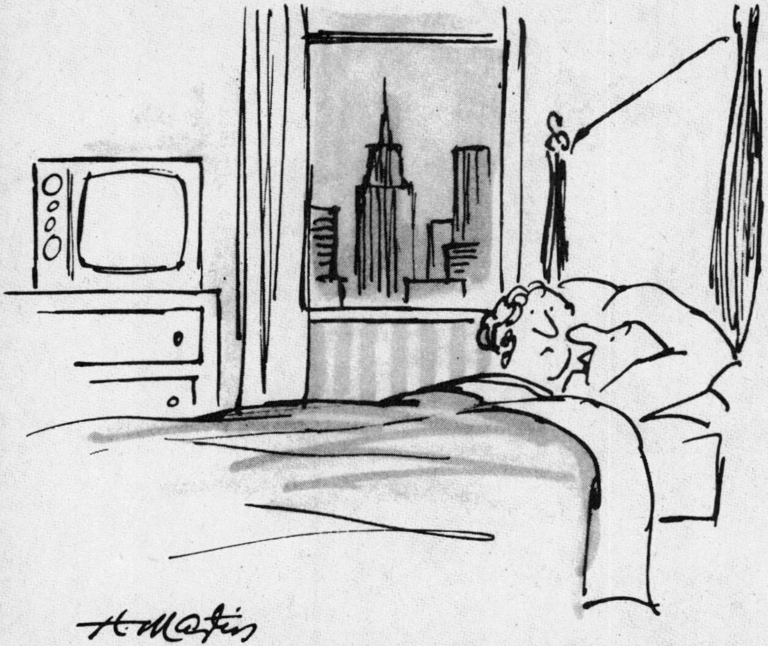

"One consolation – if there **is** a nuclear war, we won't have to hear all about it every two seconds on radio and TV."

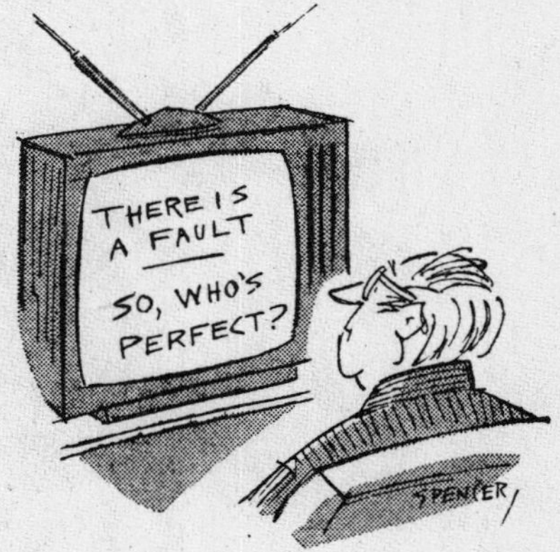

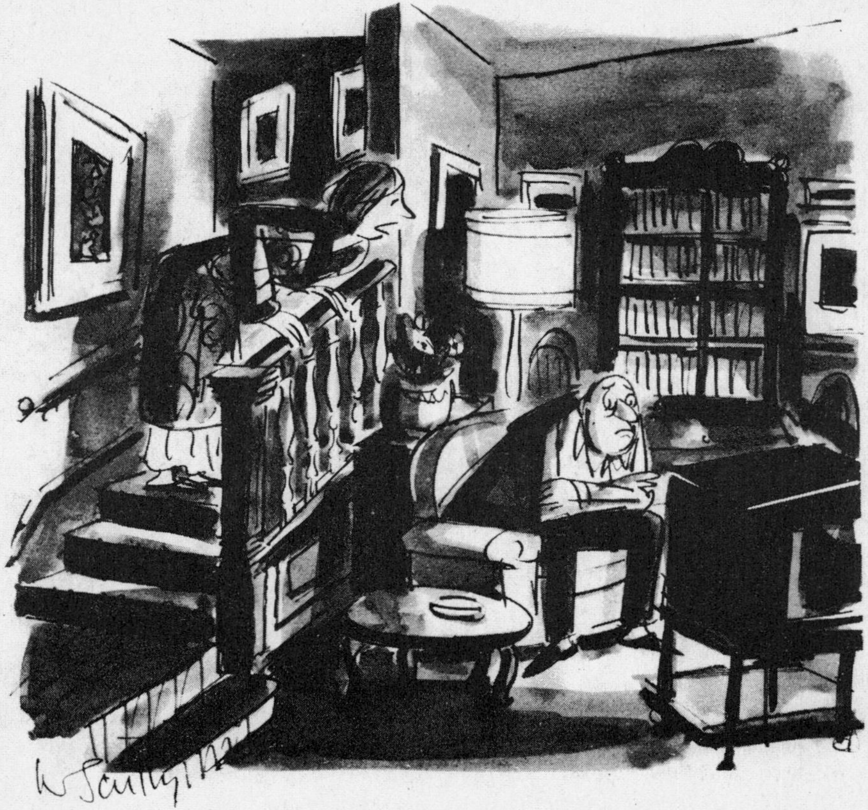

"Come to bed, dear. You've been through the mill enough for one day."

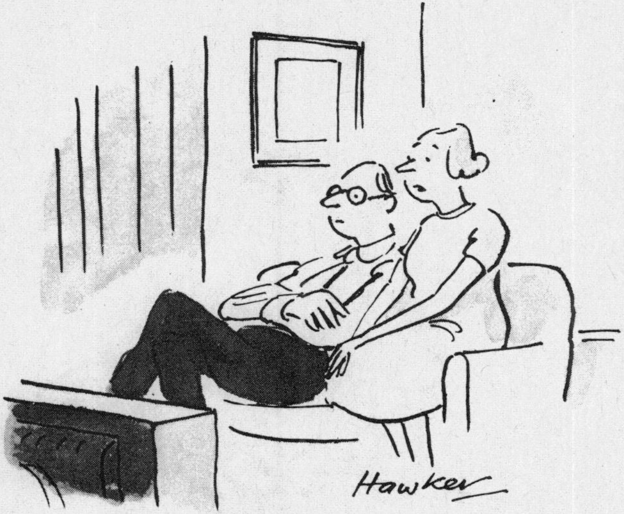

"Well, this won't get our TV supper prepared."

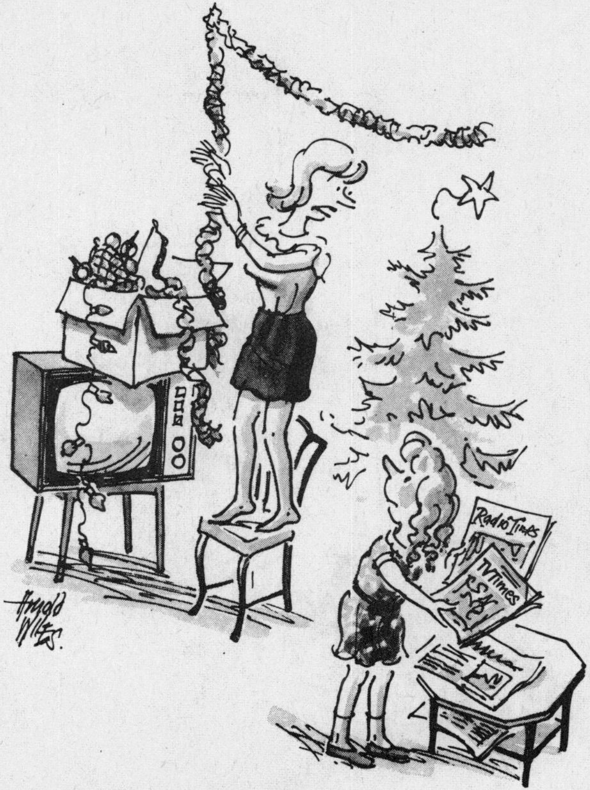

"Don't throw away the Radio or TV Times – they'll come in handy next year."

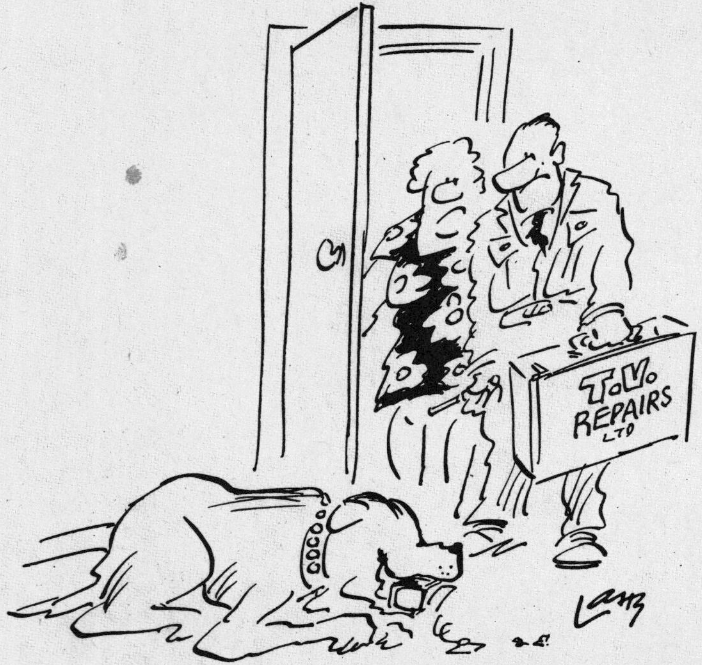
T.V. REPAIRS LTD

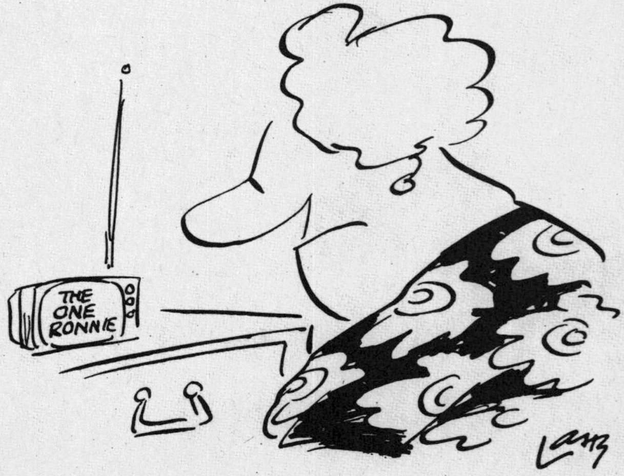
THE ONE RONNIE

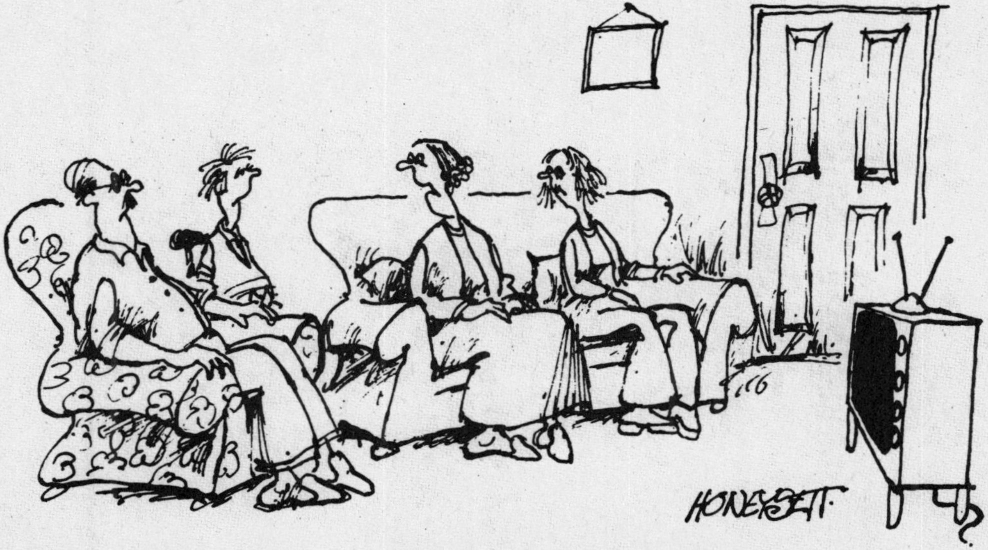

"That's the millionth time you've said it'll be a good thing for us to be without it for a few days."

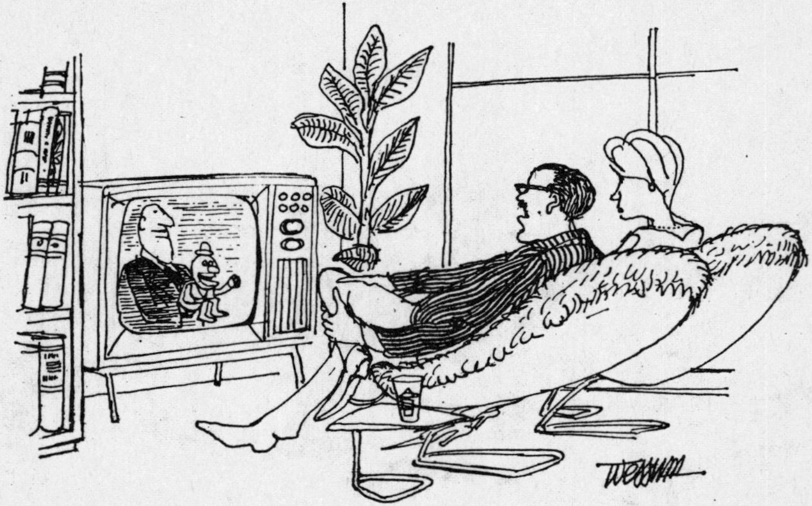

"Oh, did I tell you – the Chairman appointed a new member to the Board."

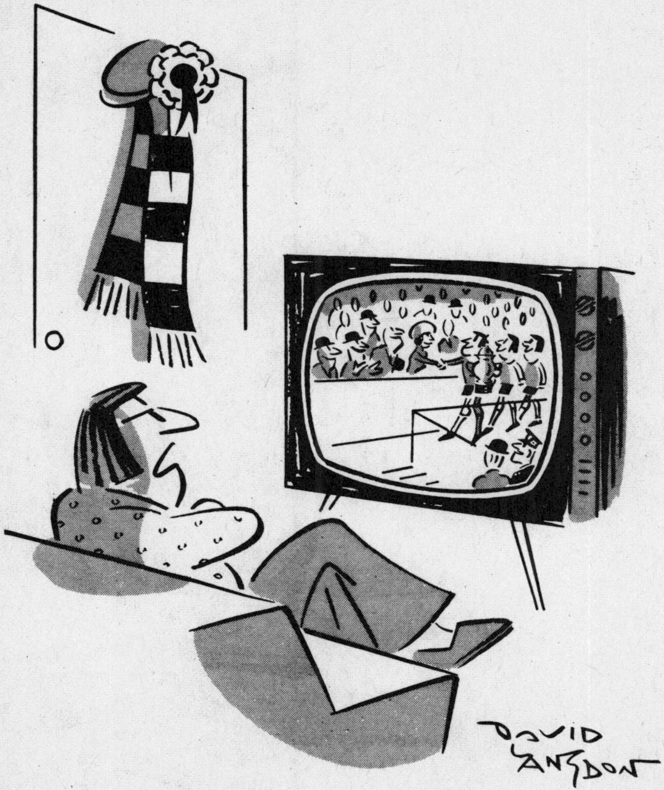

"Once-a-year soccer fans, and **I** *couldn't get a ticket."*

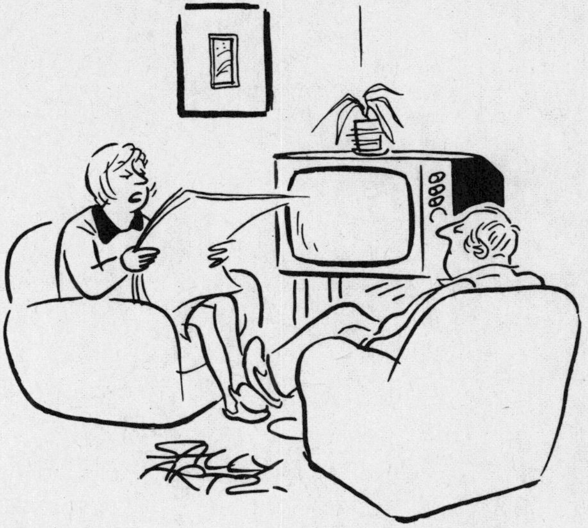

" '. . . biting social comment . . .' '. . . compulsive viewing . . .' – what's on the other channel?"

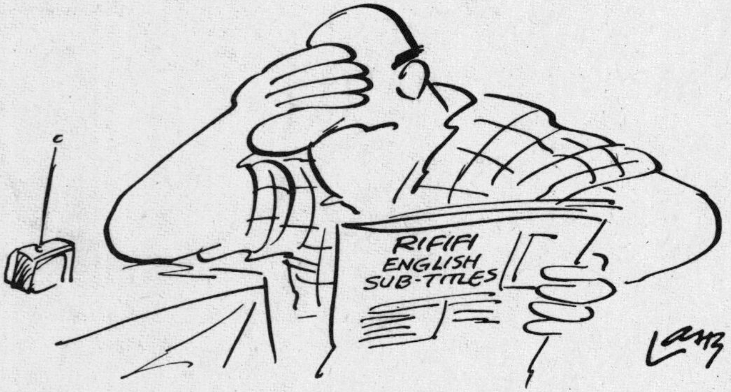
RIFIFI
ENGLISH
SUB-TITLES

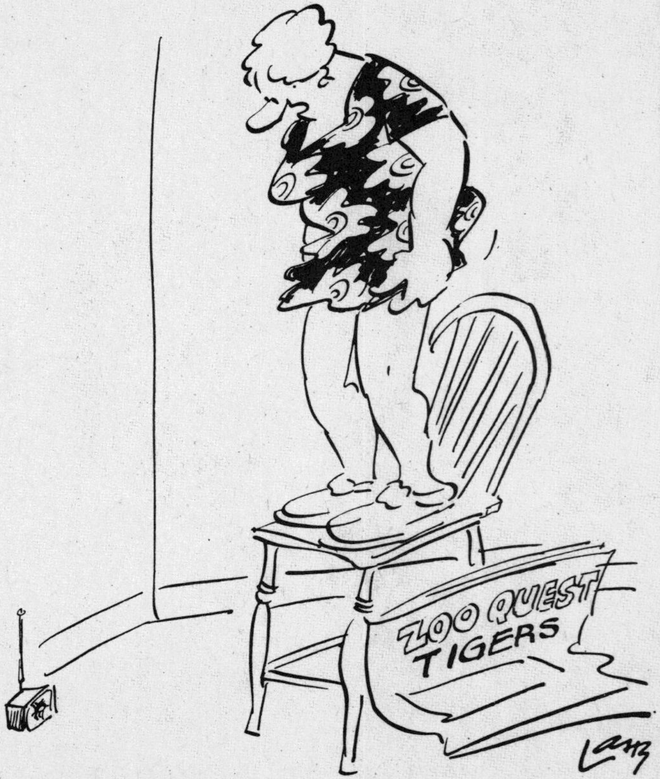
ZOO QUEST
TIGERS

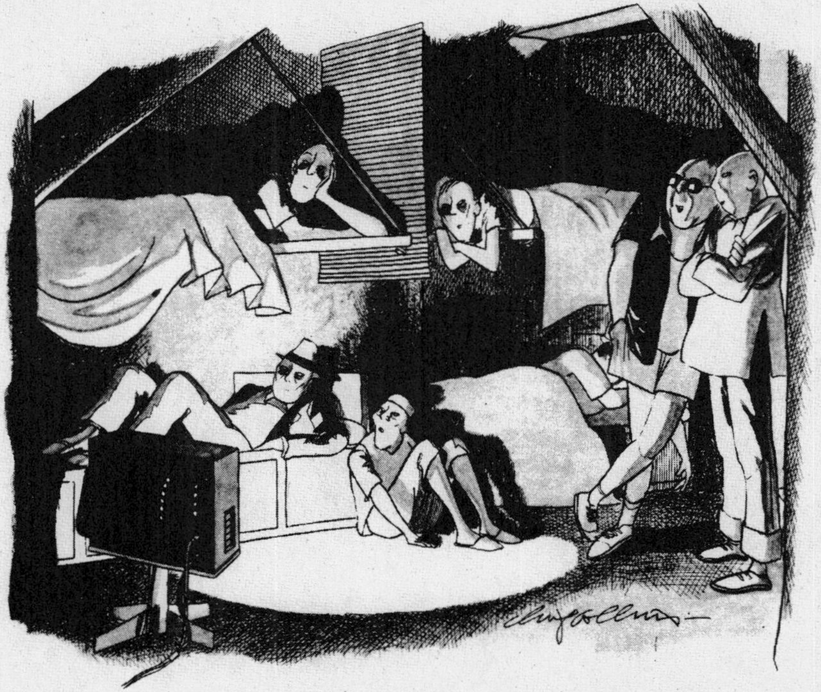

"It's cheaper . . . has roughly the same effect . . . and I get no hassles from the Drug Squad . . ."

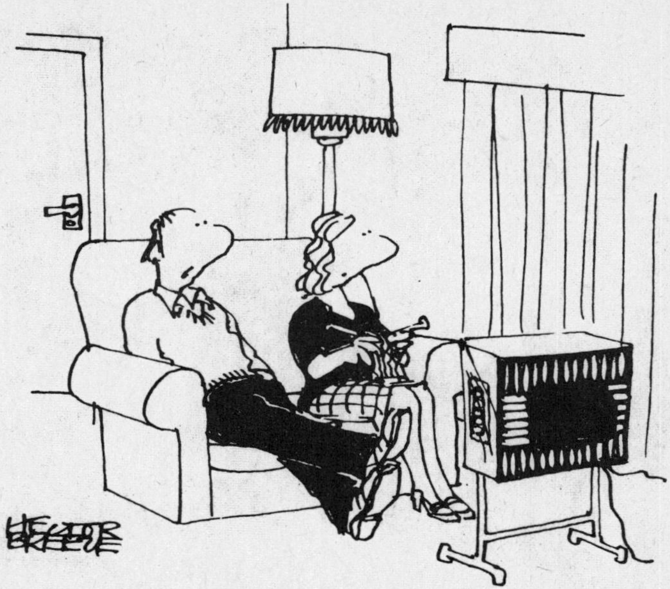

"I don't know why we haven't got the willpower to switch it off and read some spin-off books."

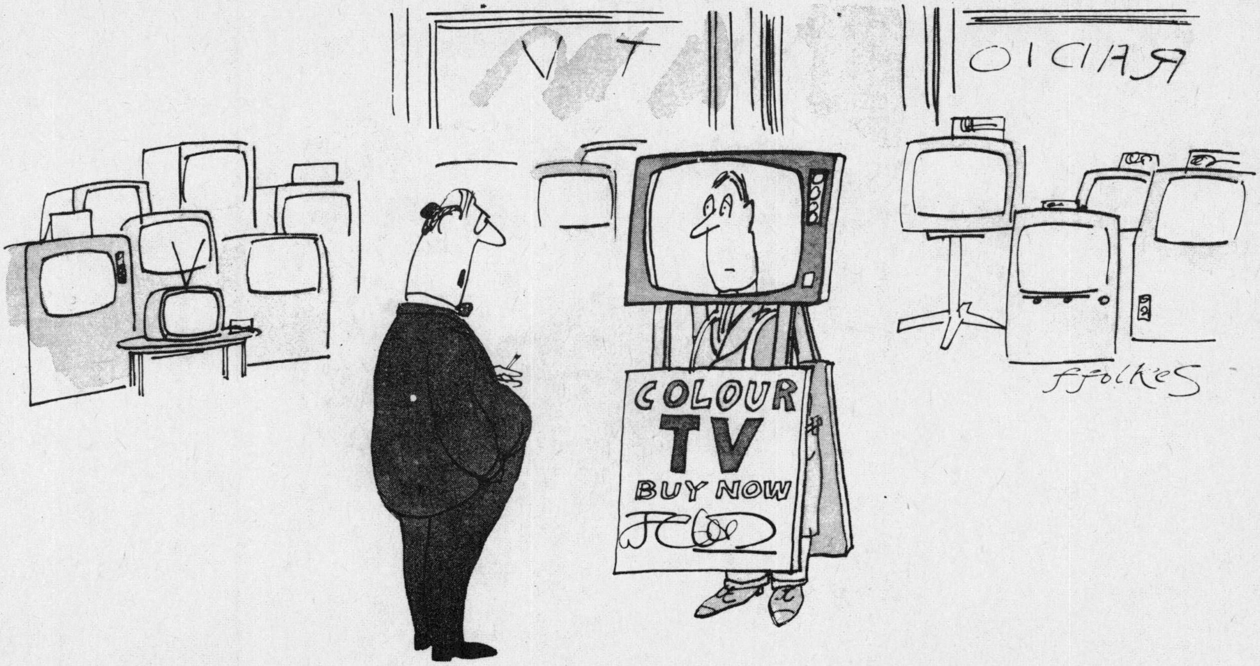

"You're terribly pale, Hoskins. Run around the block a couple of times."

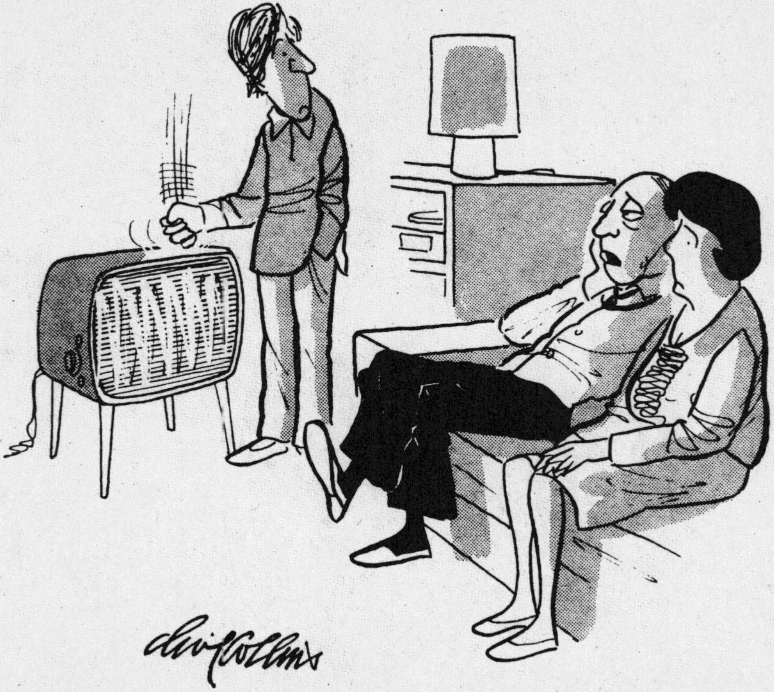

". . . three years at technical college . . . that the best you can do?"

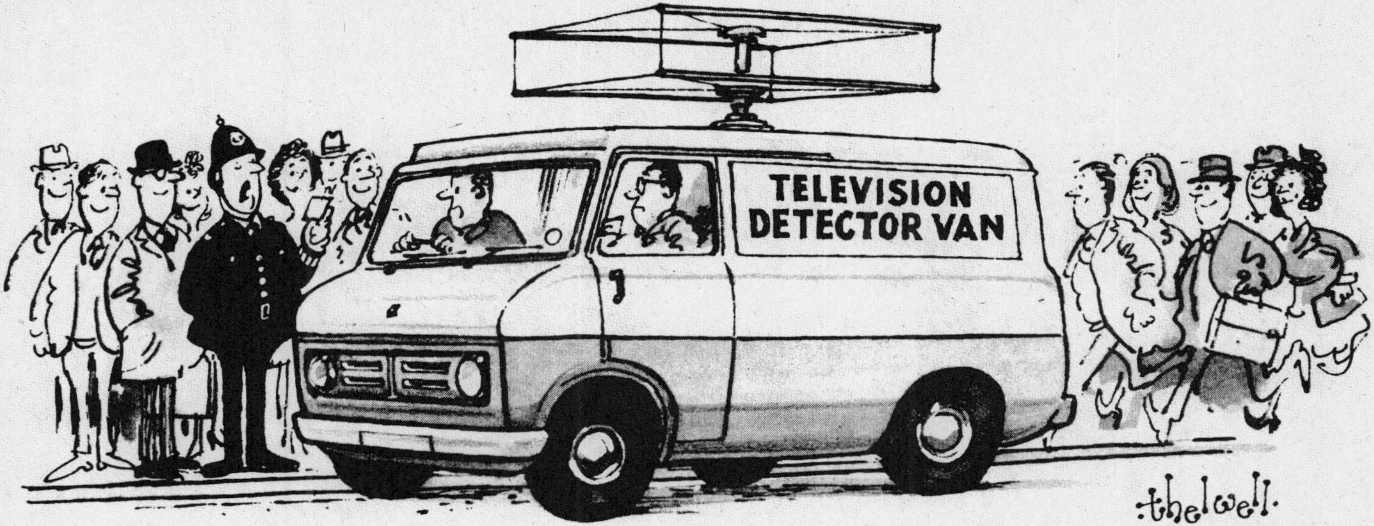

"Your licence has run out."

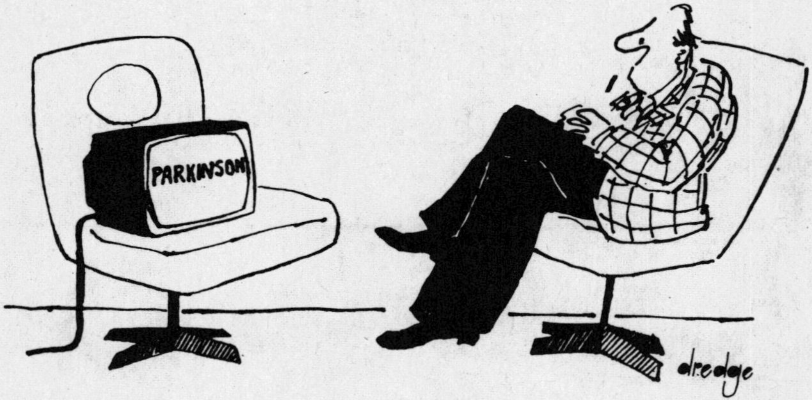
PARKINSON
dredge

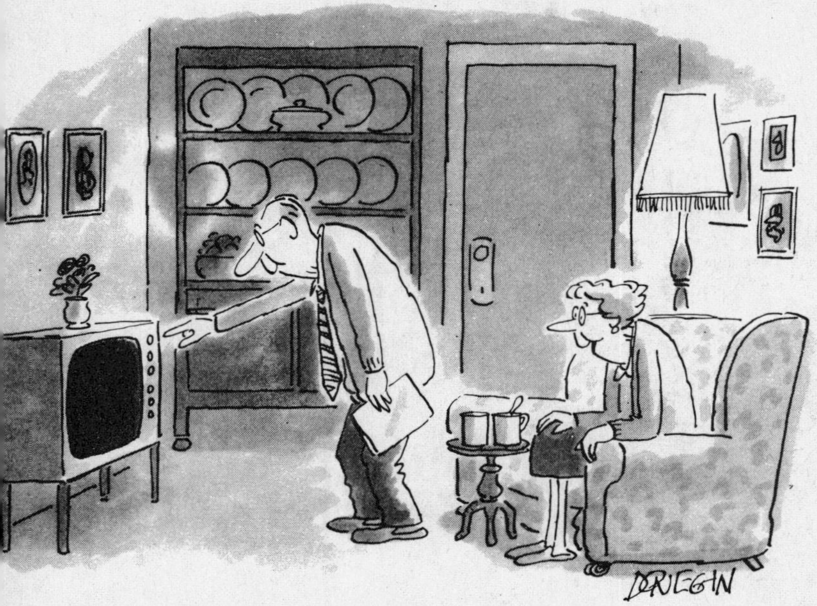

"Whoopee – here we go again!"

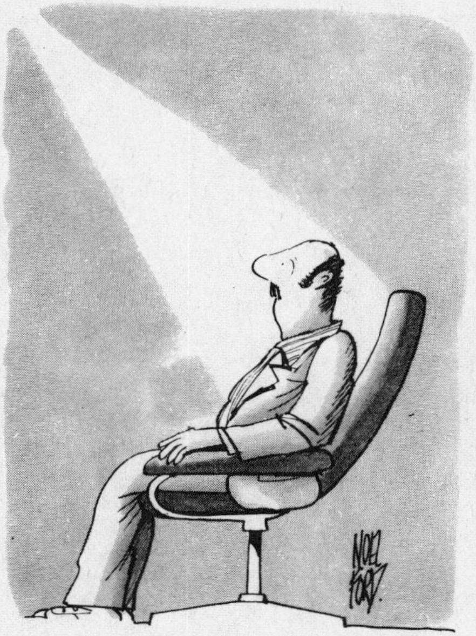

"At the end of that round on your specialist subject of English Vernacular, Mr Sturgeon, you have scored nine points. You had four passes, two 'Buggered if I know thats' and one 'Stone me mate, what d'yer fink I am, a flamin' Encyclo-bleedin' paedia?' "

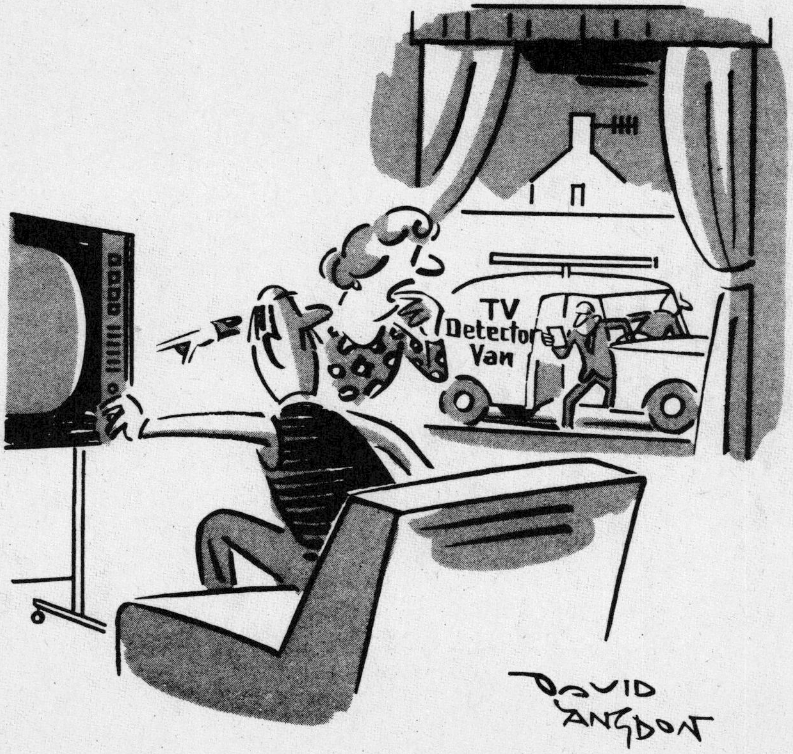

"Oh, my God, here they come – at least tune it down to black and white!"

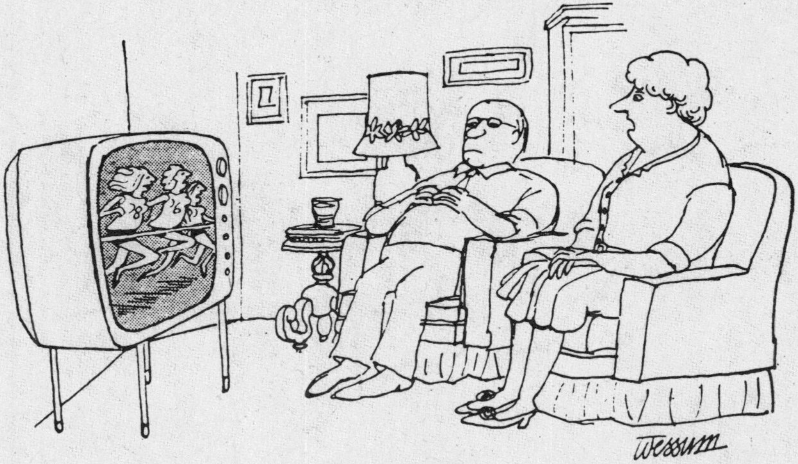

"Yes, but I can make a bed in 43.9 seconds."

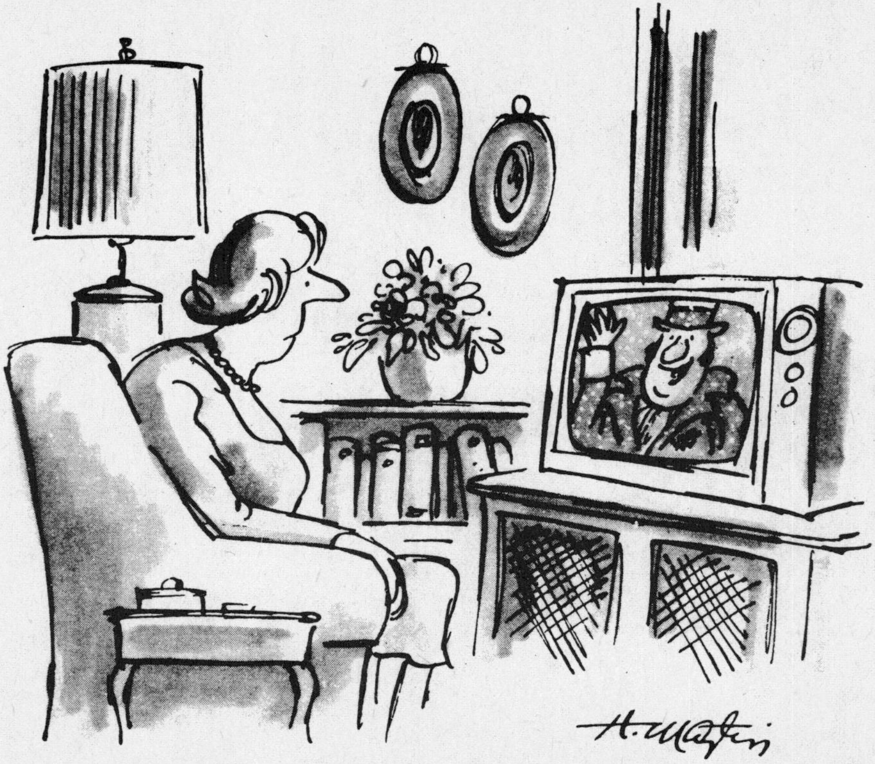

"The makers of Sno-Glo want to wish you warm season's greetings and happiness in the New Year. The cost of this fifteen-second spot announcement is hidden in the purchase price of your next box of Sno-Glo. Thank you and God bless you."

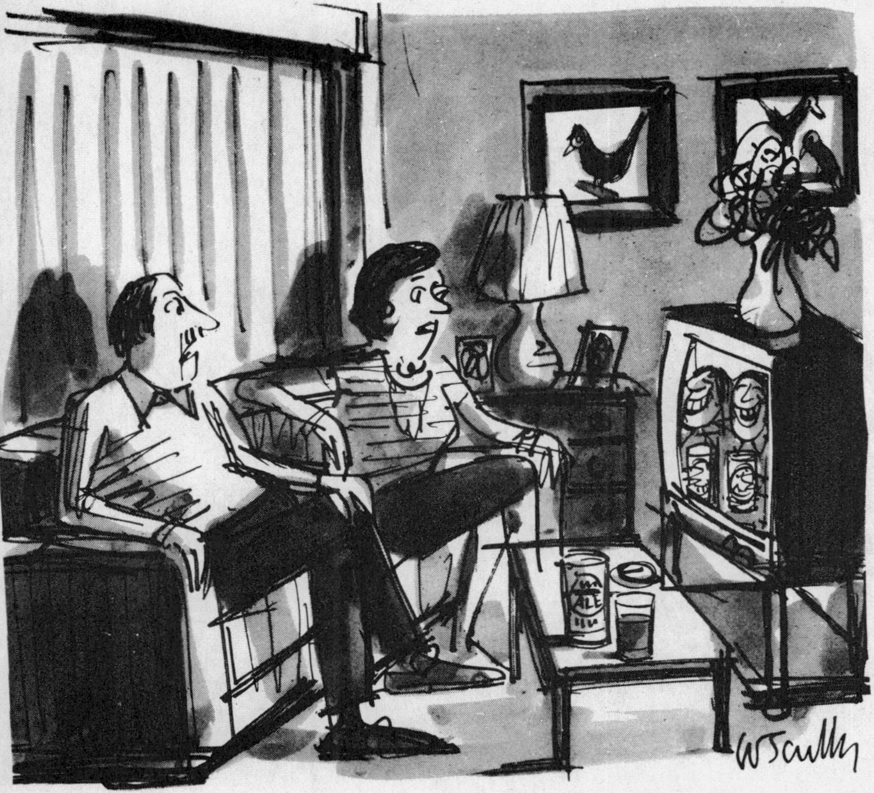

"What I can't stand is those yobbos drinking my particular brand of beer."

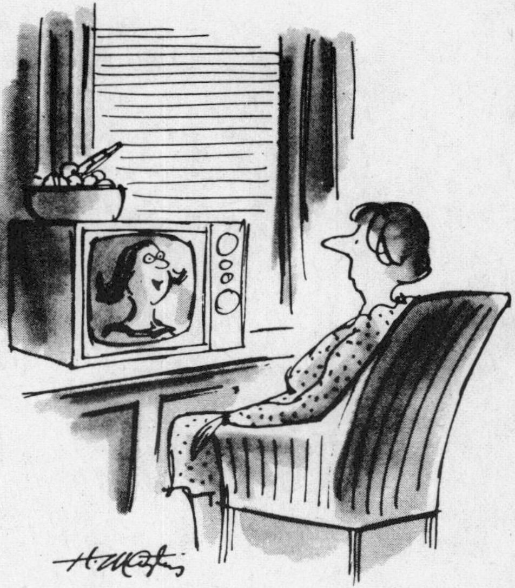

"As you know this is the last show of the series. Since we have not been renewed for next year we thought we'd gather the cast and just tell you a little about ourselves, our plans for the future, who gets along with who, who smokes pot, who has a drinking problem, who's sleeping with who . . ."

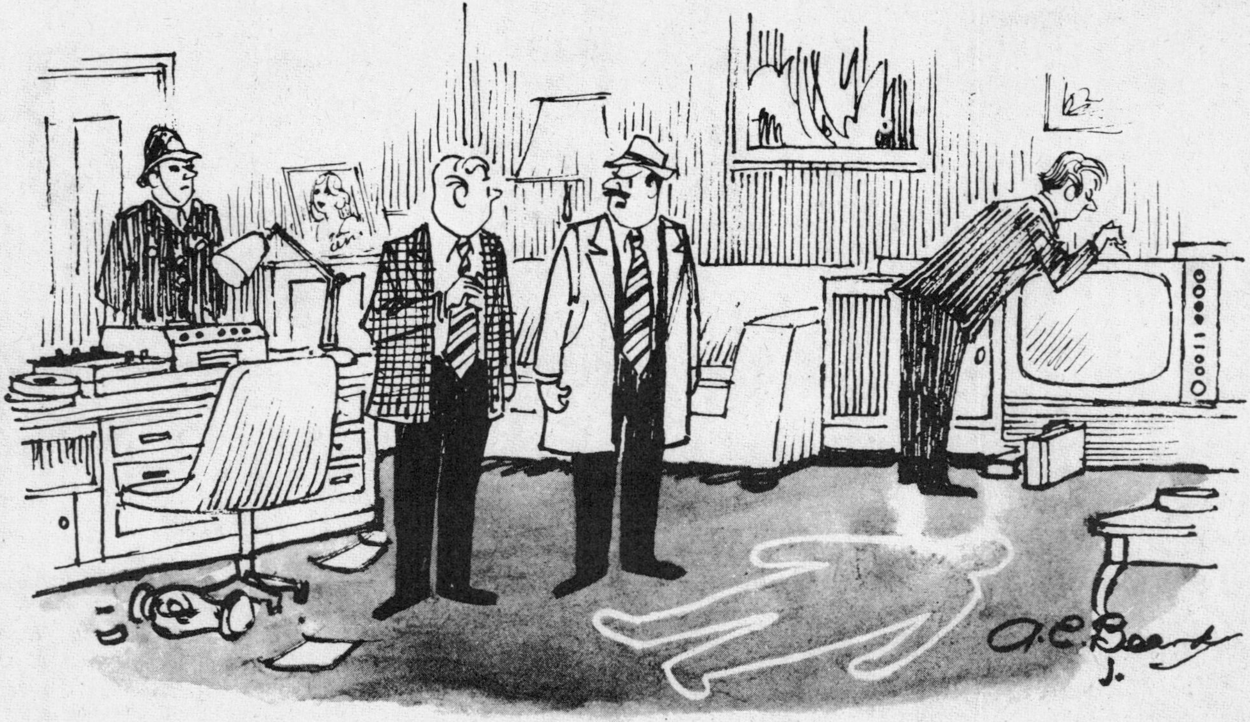

"I'm quite aware he was a television chat show personality, Sergeant, but we'd better look for some other motive."

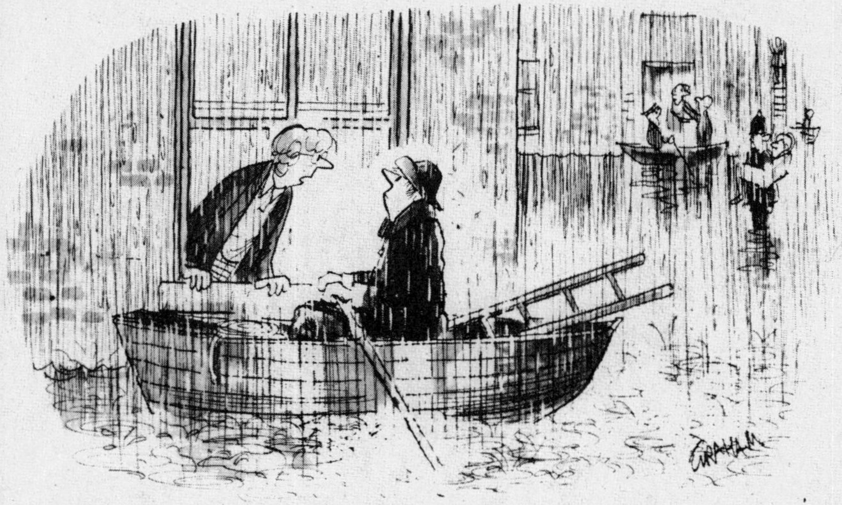

"Are you the man come to repair the television?"

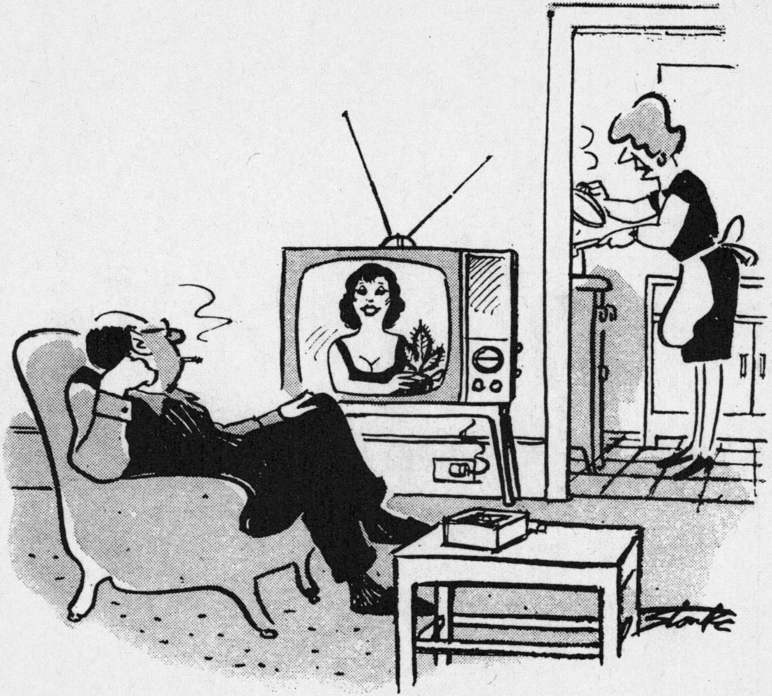

"I shouldn't have thought that a talk about the rock plants of Patagonia was ***your*** *cup of tea."*

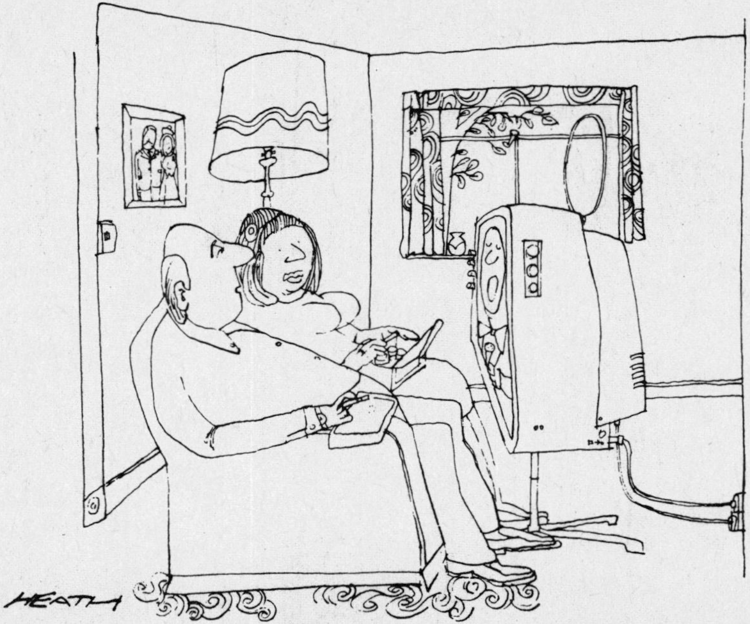

"Is he making a comeback, or is it a repeat?"

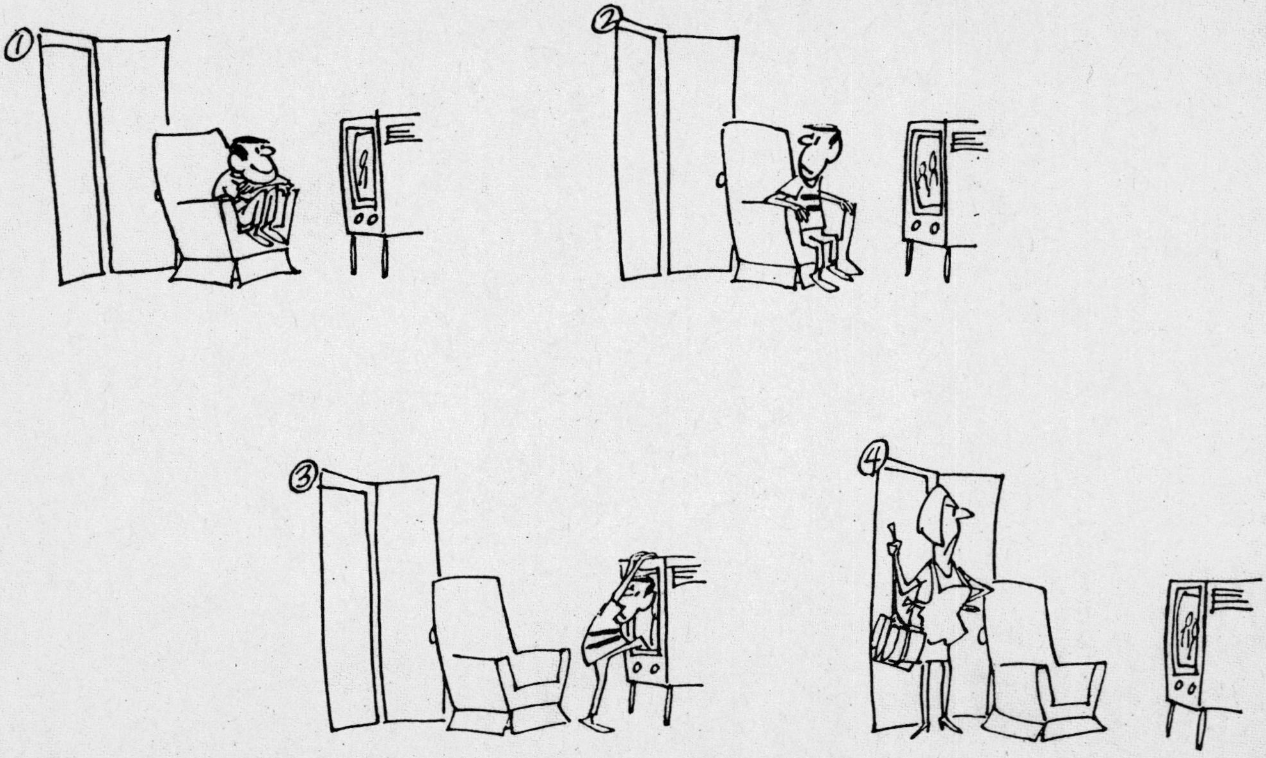

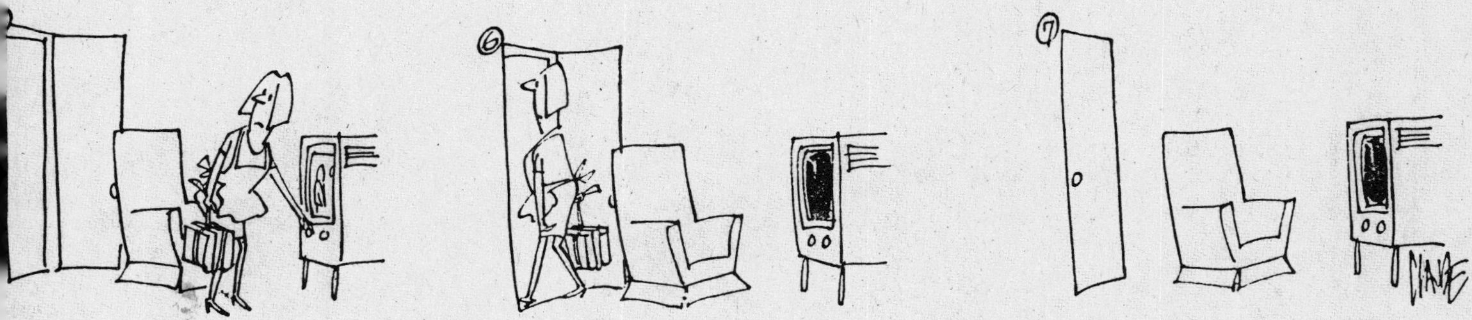
6
7

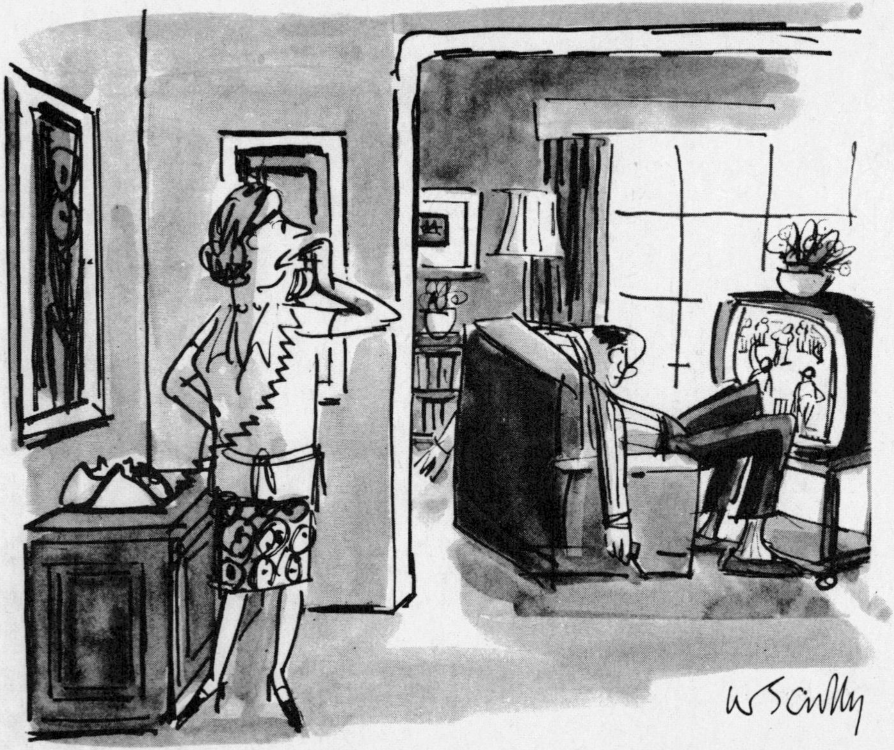

"I'm afraid it's impossible to get him to the 'phone – he's riveted to the box."

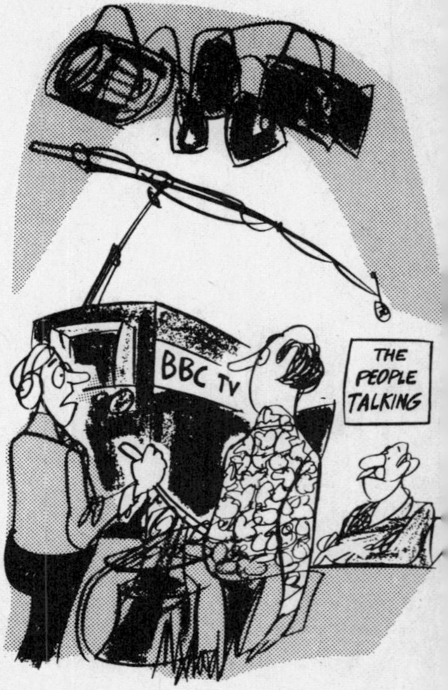

"Tell me again, I've forgotten which way we're supposed to be biased?"

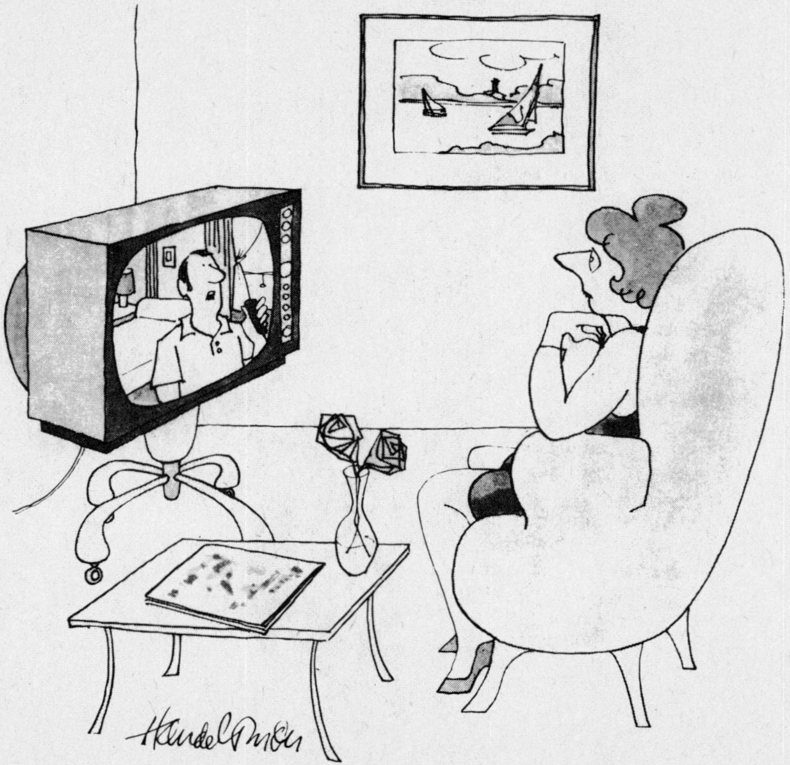

"The authorities have denied permission to film the actual street fighting. I have, however, obtained clearance to show you my room at the Hilton, and here it is."

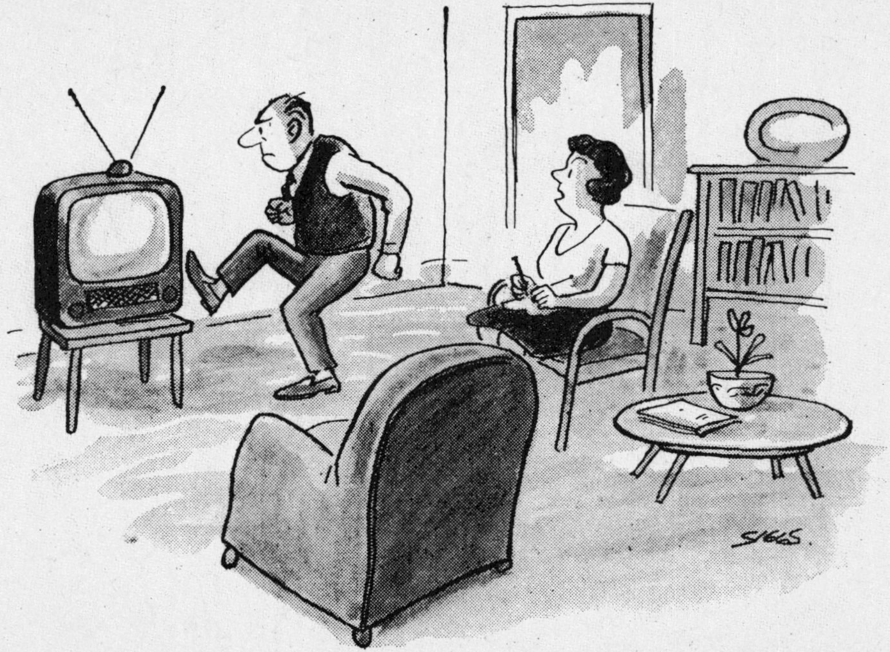

"It said 'Do not adjust your set,' Fred."

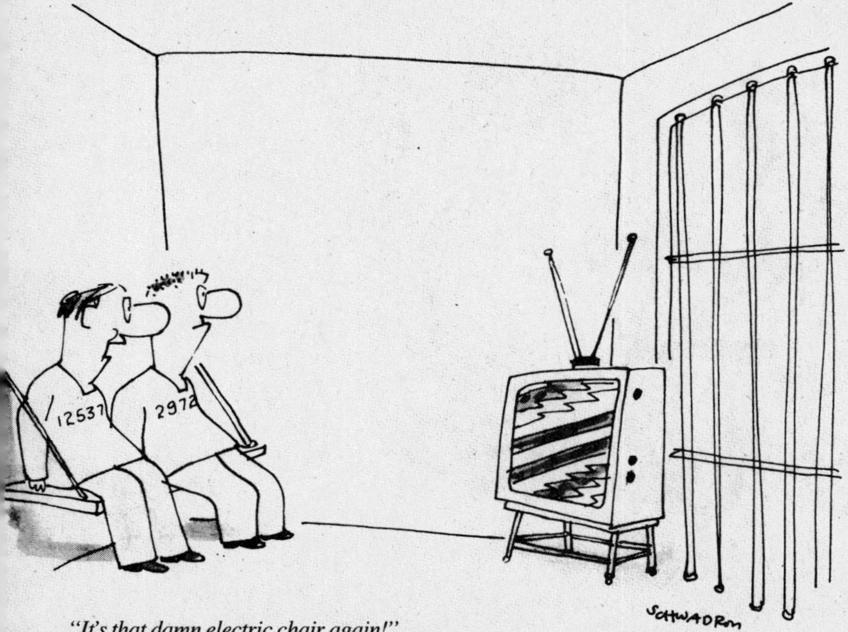

"It's that damn electric chair again!"

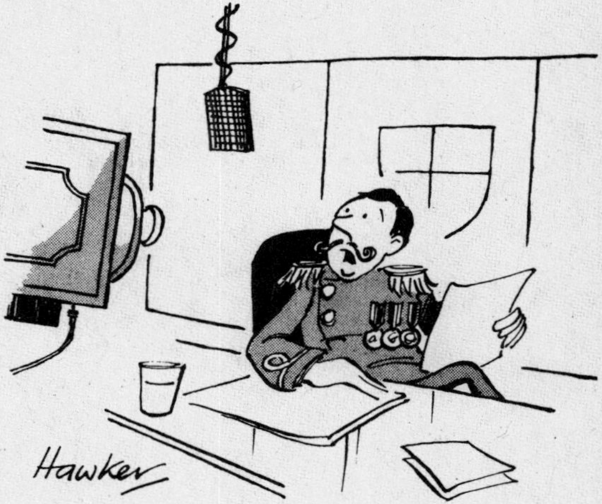

"Tonight looks like being a pretty good night for you solemn music fans . . ."

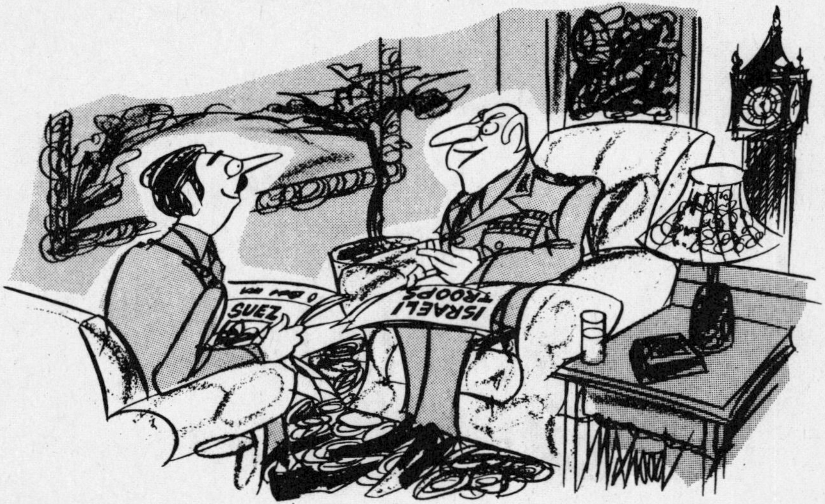

"There I was, doing a little reconnaissance of the situation on 'The World at One', reserving my main assault for 'Panorama', while keeping something in reserve for 'News Extra'."

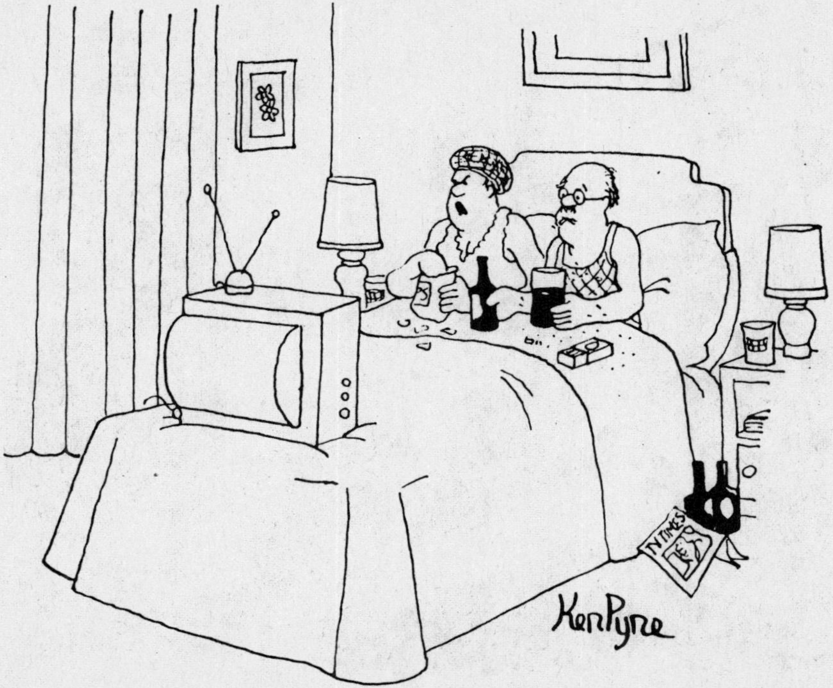

"I don't think the bedroom scenes are very convincing!"

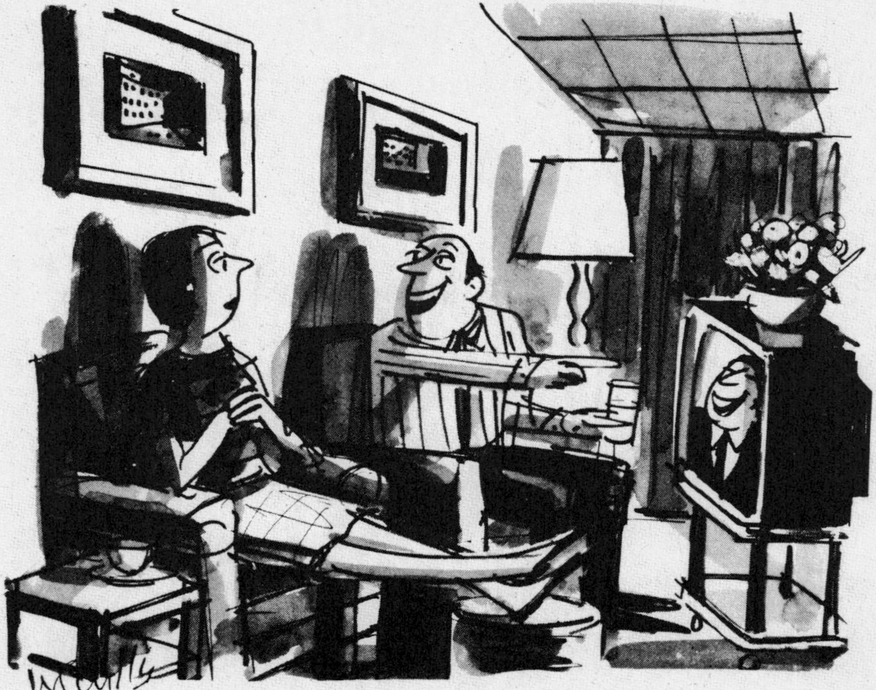

"Ha, Ha! That was an in-joke – the giggle-track people didn't see it."

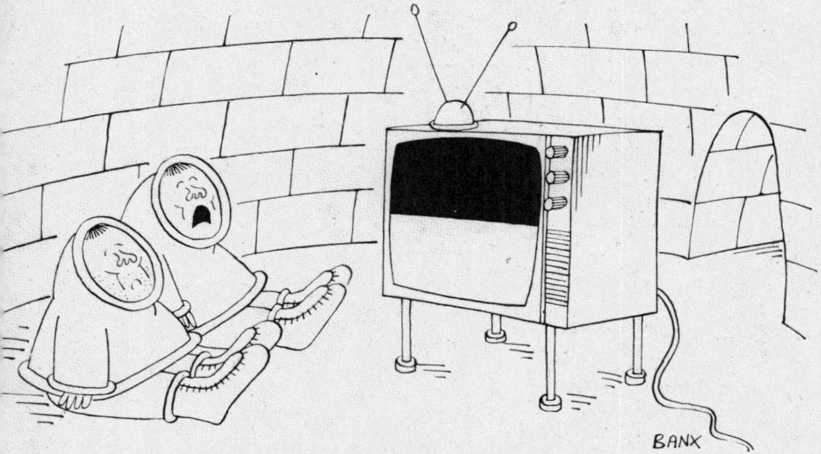

"I wish they wouldn't film **everything** on bloody location, that's all."

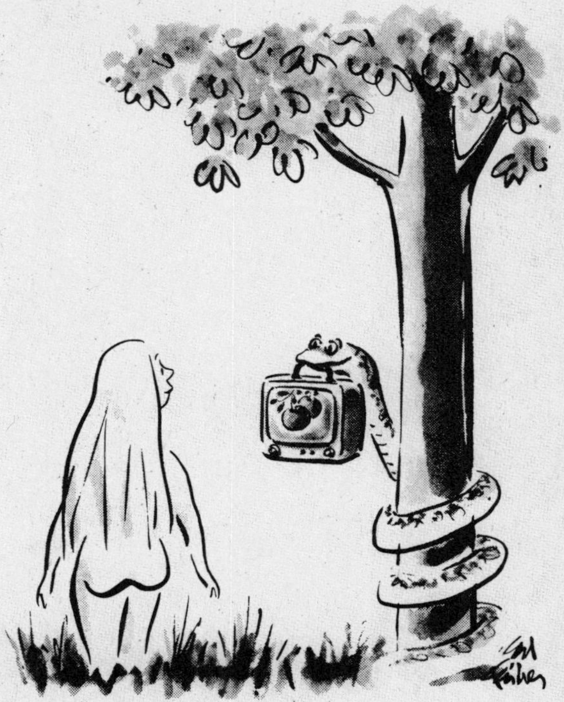

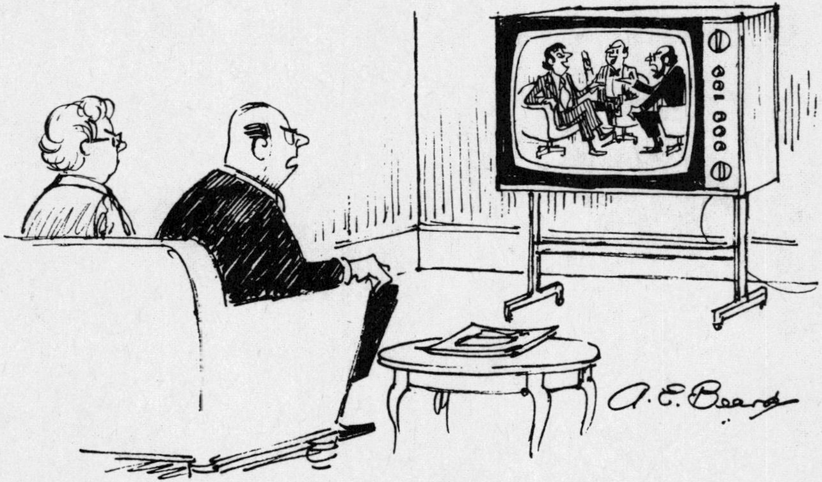

"Conversation is killing the art of television."

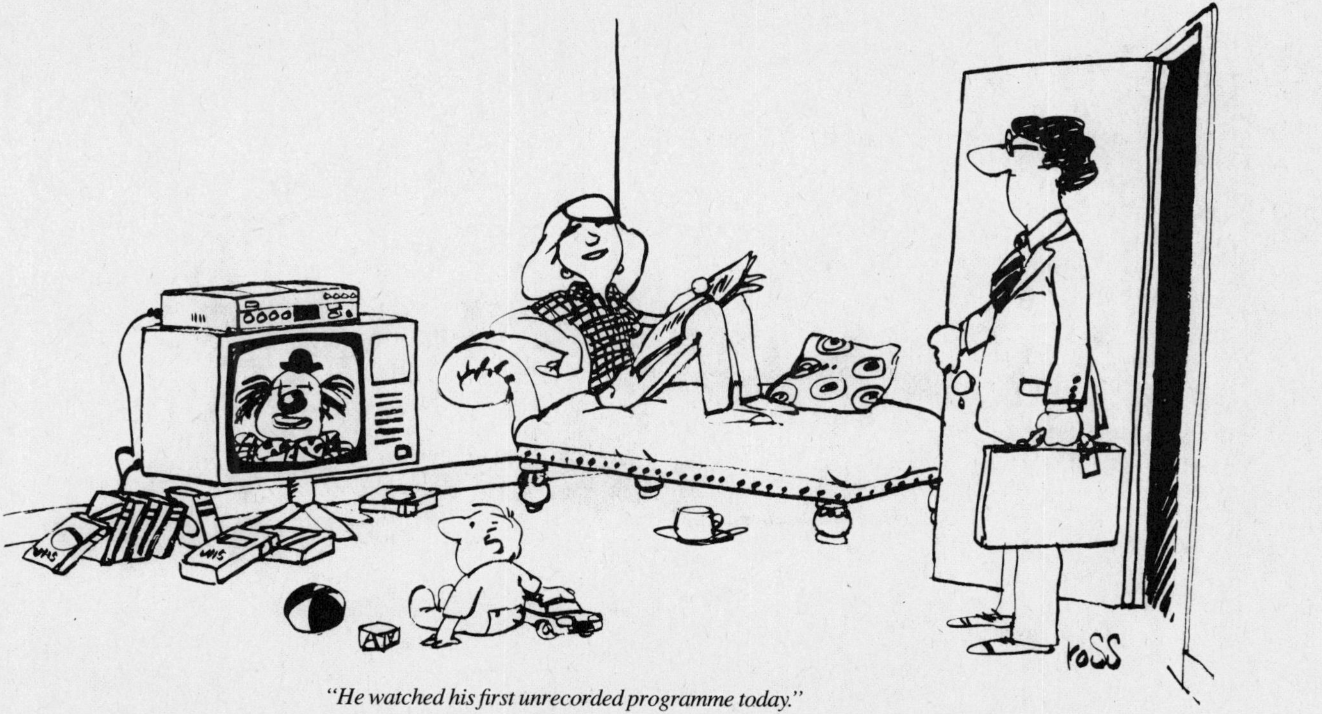

"He watched his first unrecorded programme today."

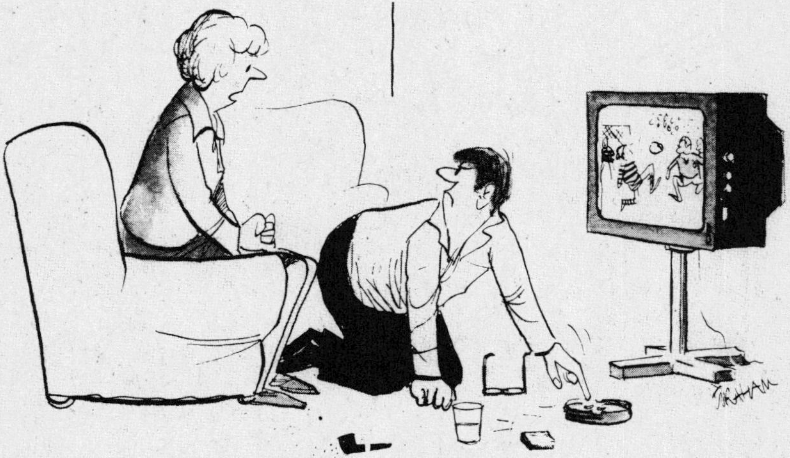

"Sid, I wish you wouldn't bother trying to explain the offside rule."

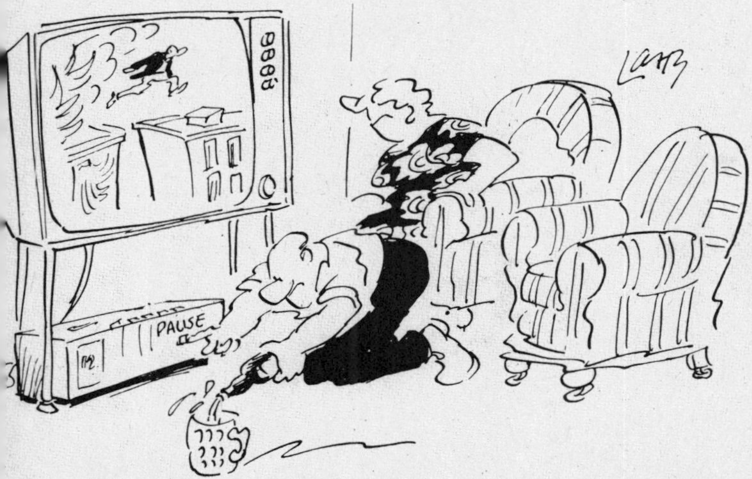
PAUSE

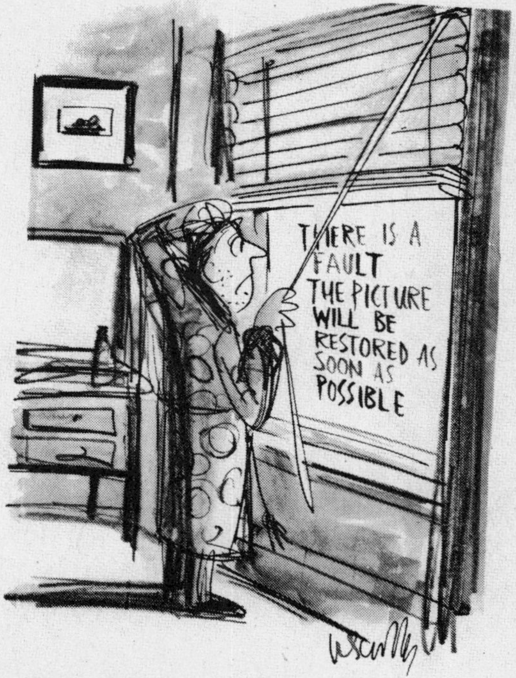
THERE IS A FAULT THE PICTURE WILL BE RESTORED AS SOON AS POSSIBLE

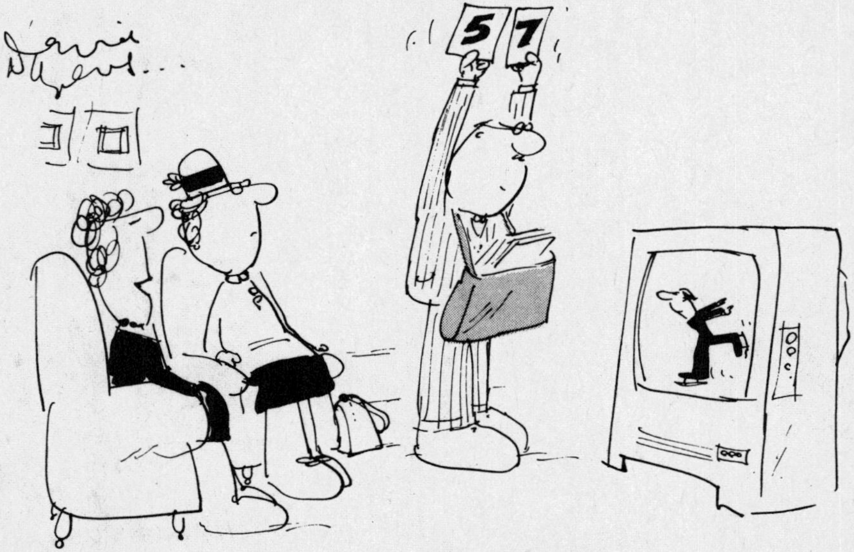

"George prefers to make his own judgement."

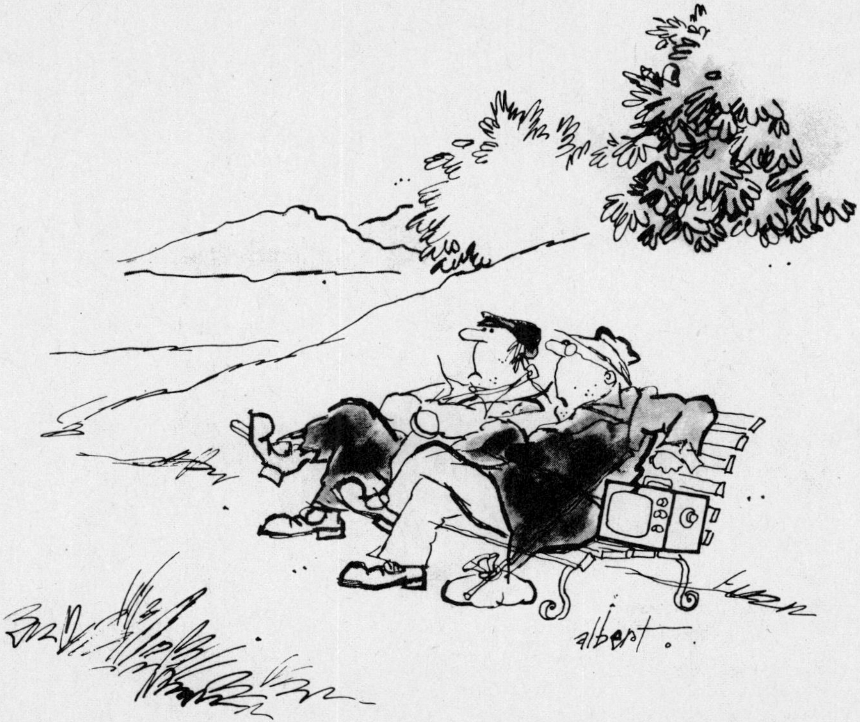

"I've wanted to escape from the materialistic rat race for a long time, but I couldn't afford a portable telly."

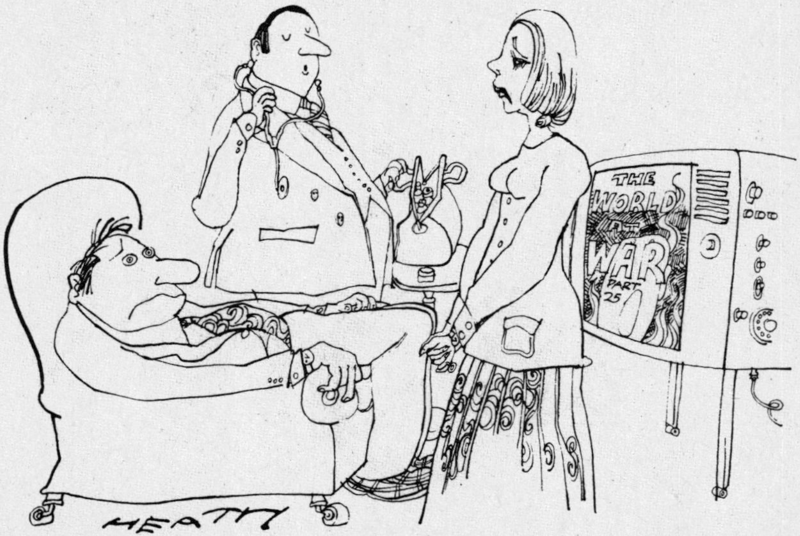

"Shellshock."

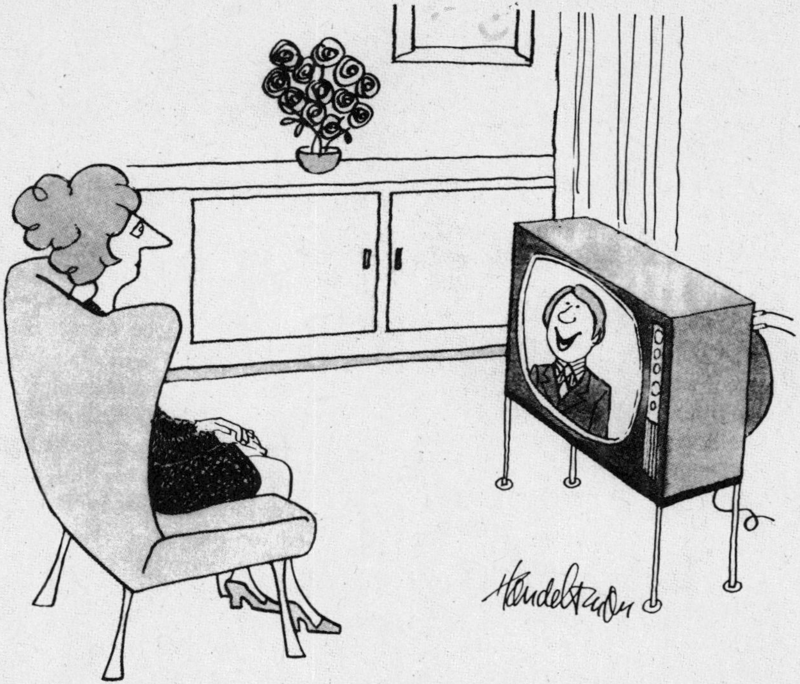

"Now don't you worry about a thing! Just sit back and let us waste your evening for you."

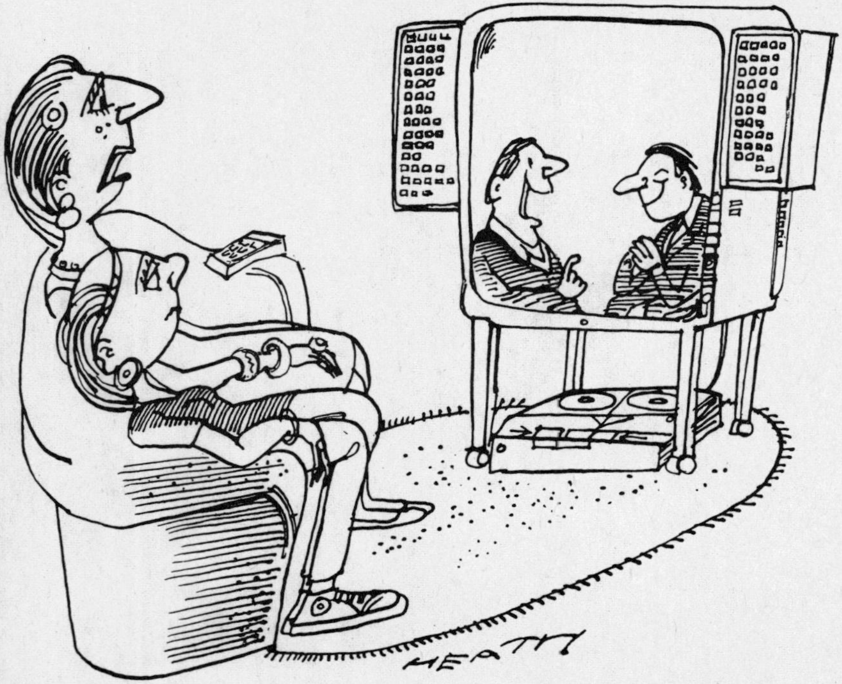

"It's funny, really – when your father's at home he never says a word."

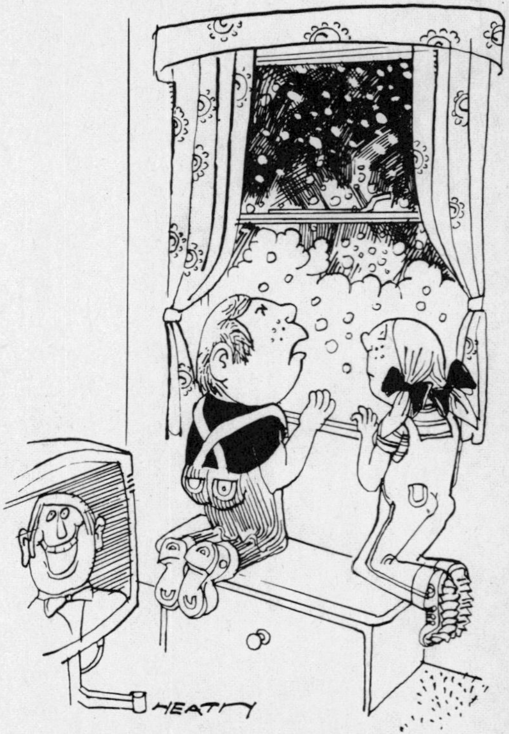

"What a drag, it's in black an' white!"

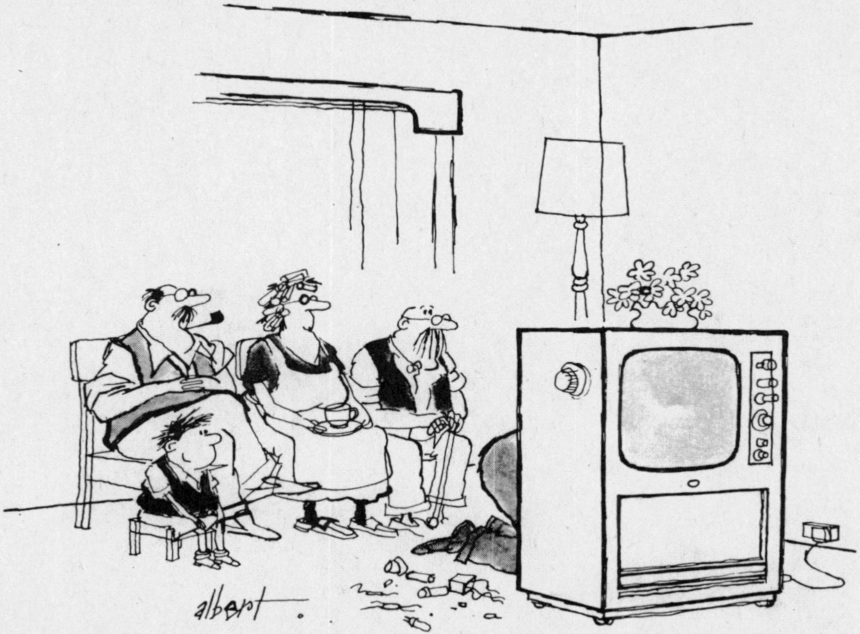
albert

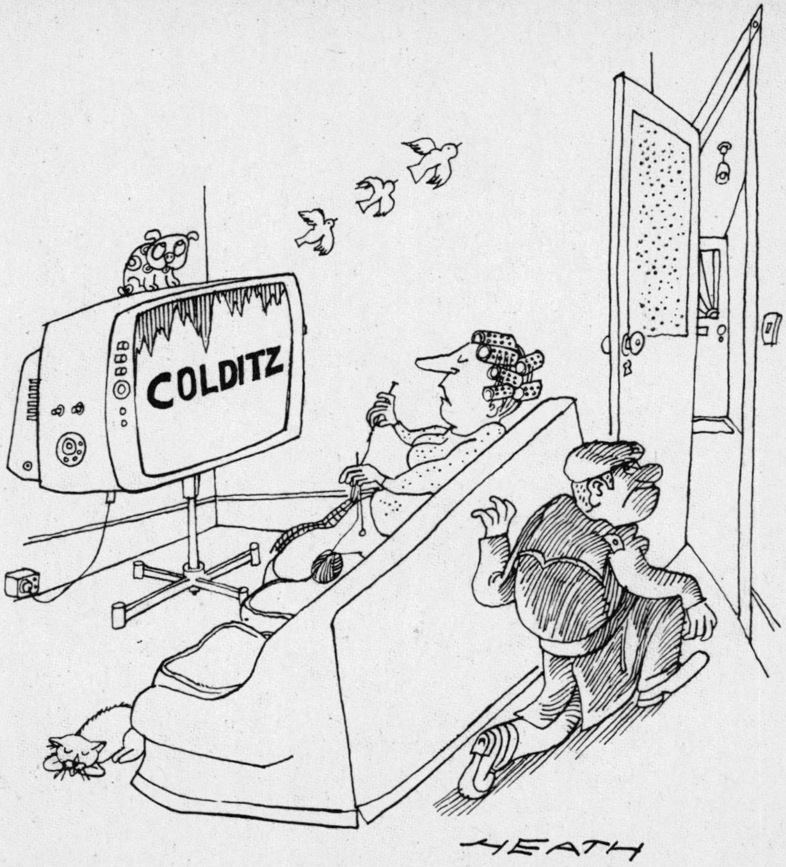

"So ze British swine thinks he's going to escape to ze British pub, does he?"

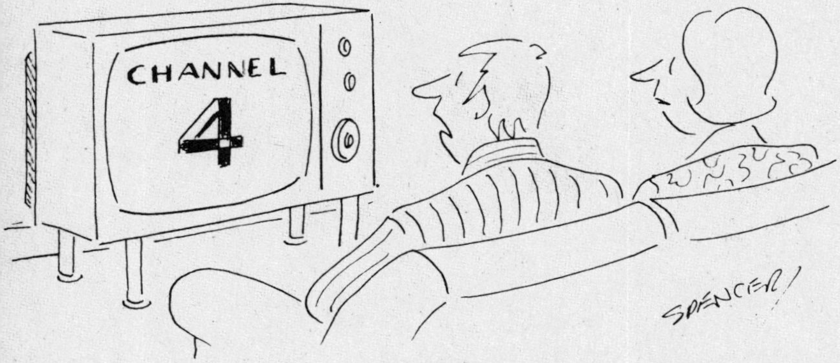

"Beats me how a channel watched by five per cent of the population can offend ninety-five per cent."

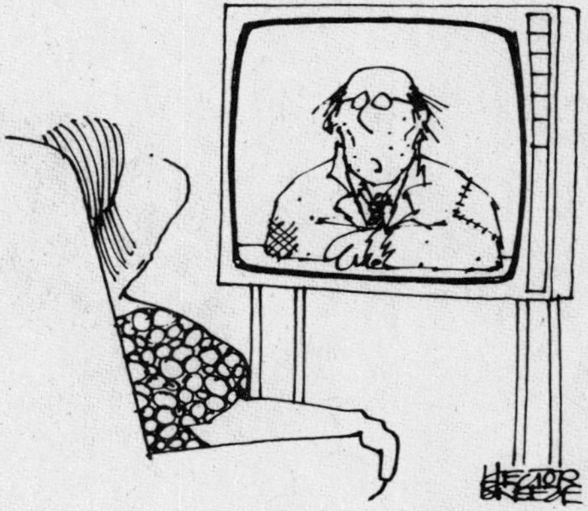

"And now for the latest news on the economic front . . ."

"She only switches it on for the chap with the gong. Then she switches it off."

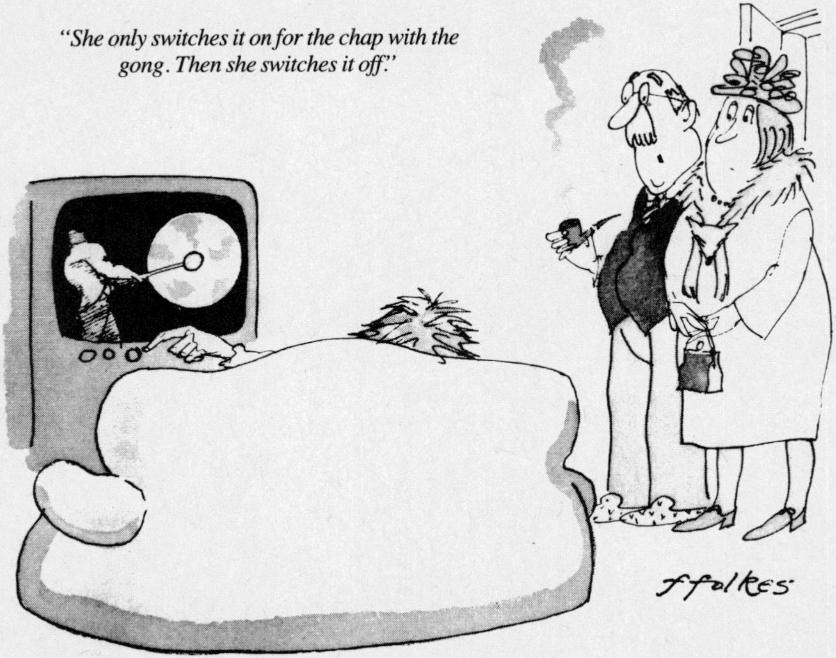

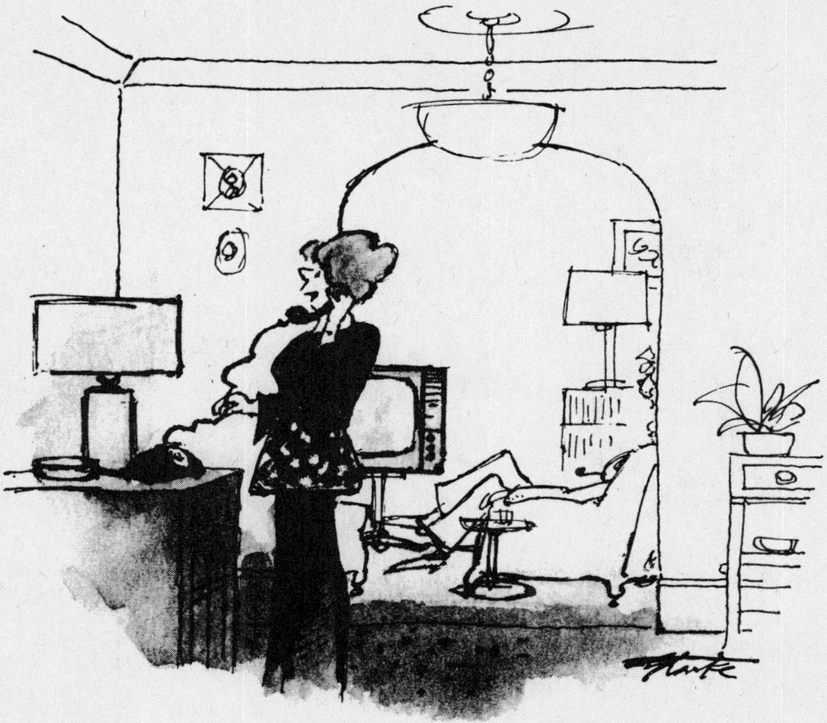

"... and how's life with YOU ... what are YOU watching?"

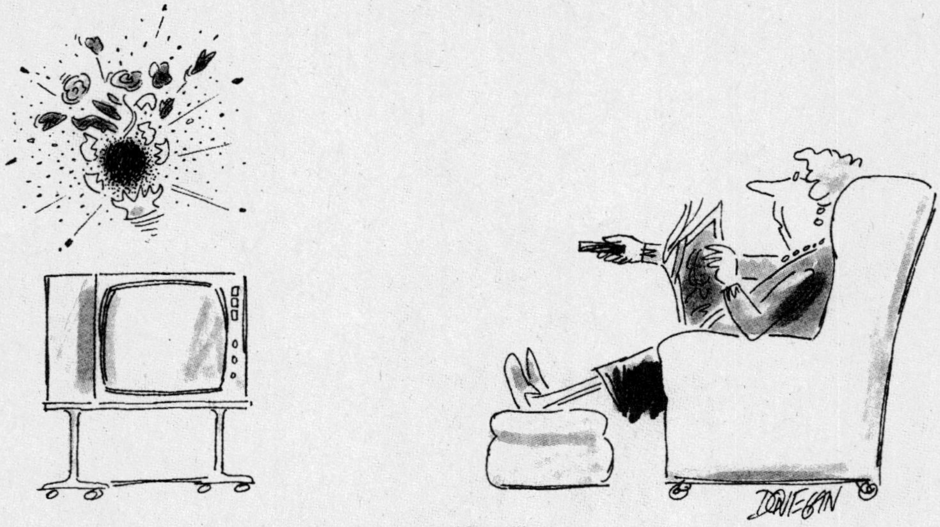

"Oops!"

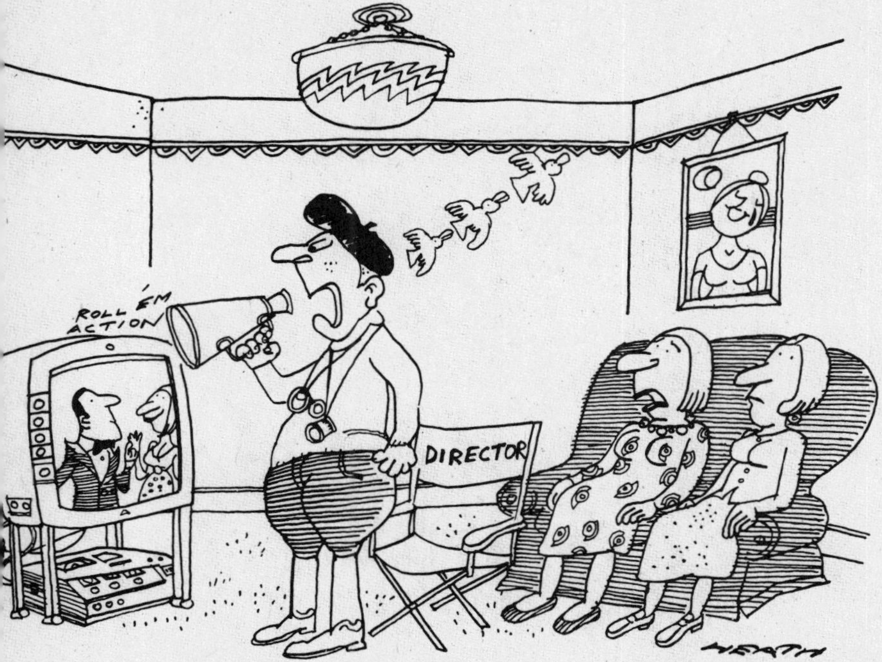

"It all started when he bought the video."

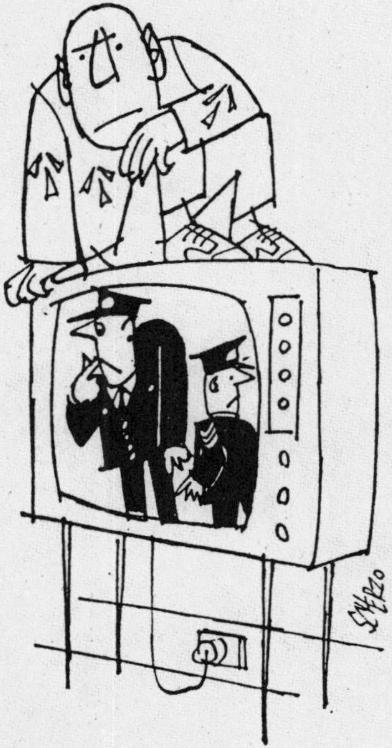

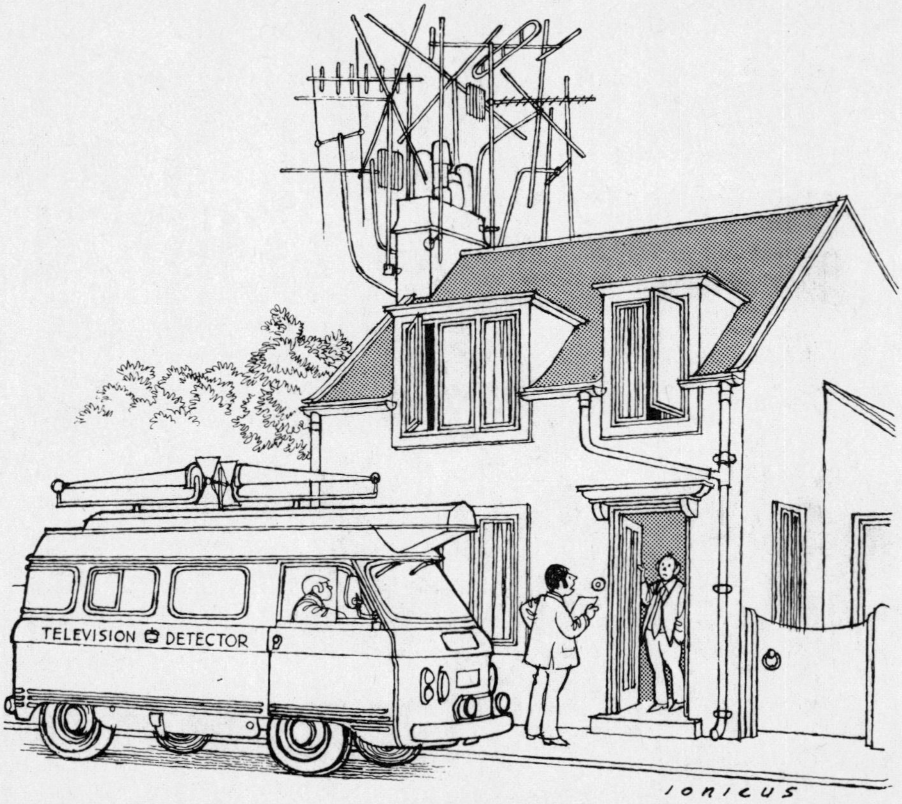

"We have reason to believe you are operating a television receiver..."

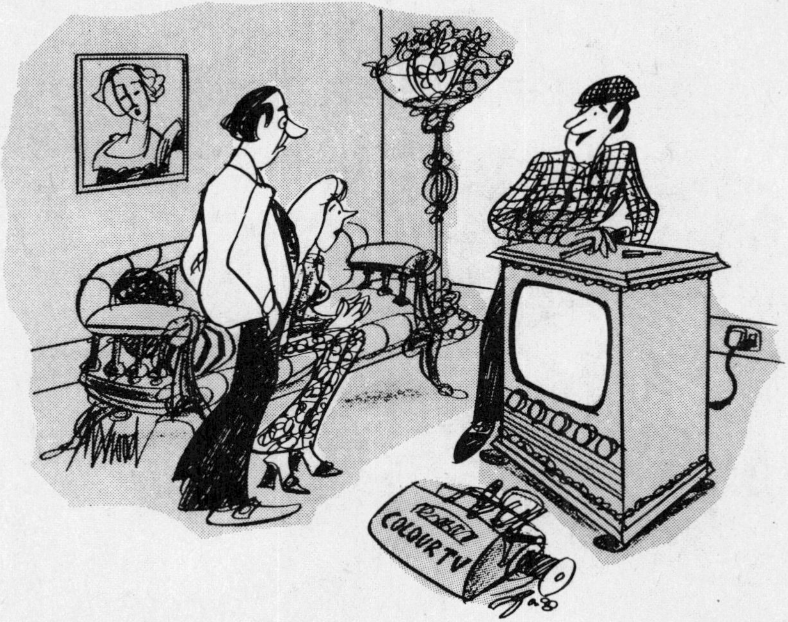

"How would you like your politicians – highly coloured, subtly pastel toned or a true life drab grey?"

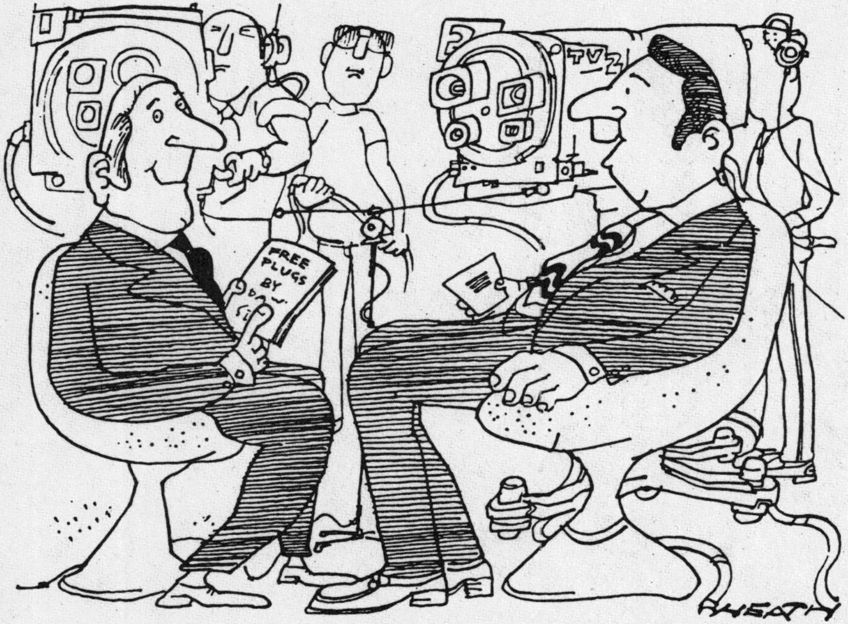

"I understand you've written a book
on how to get free plugs on television."

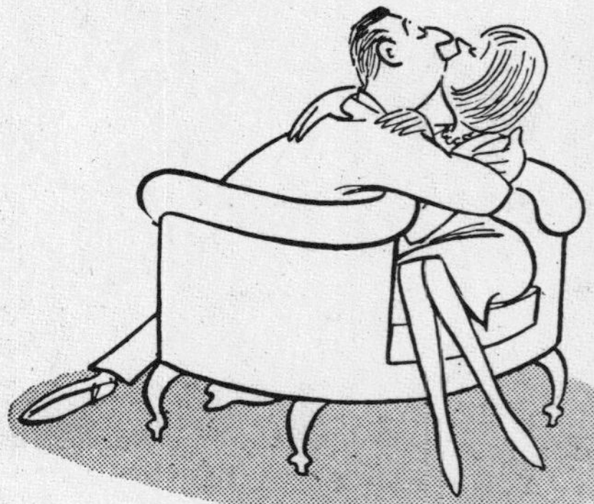

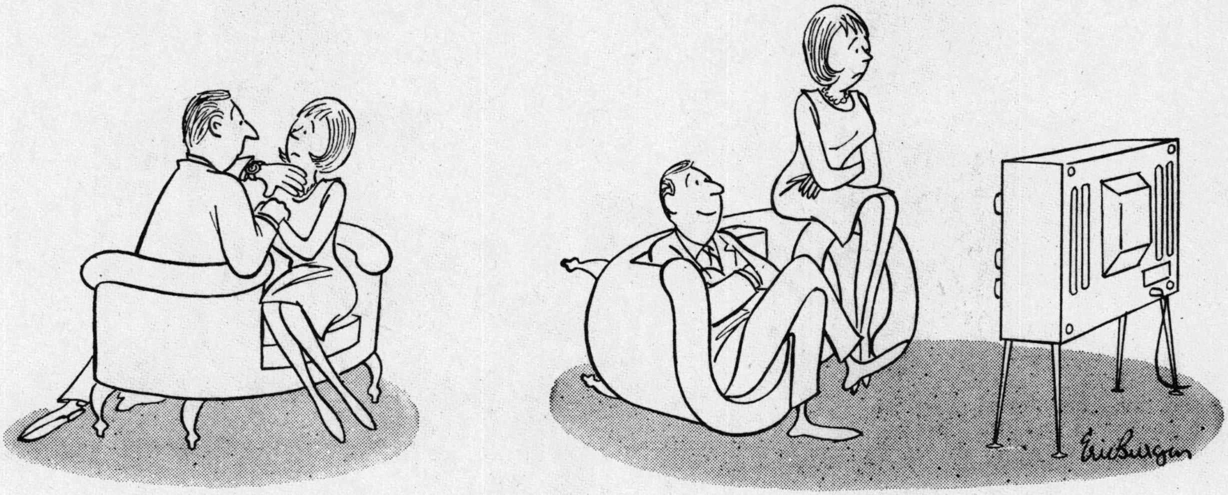

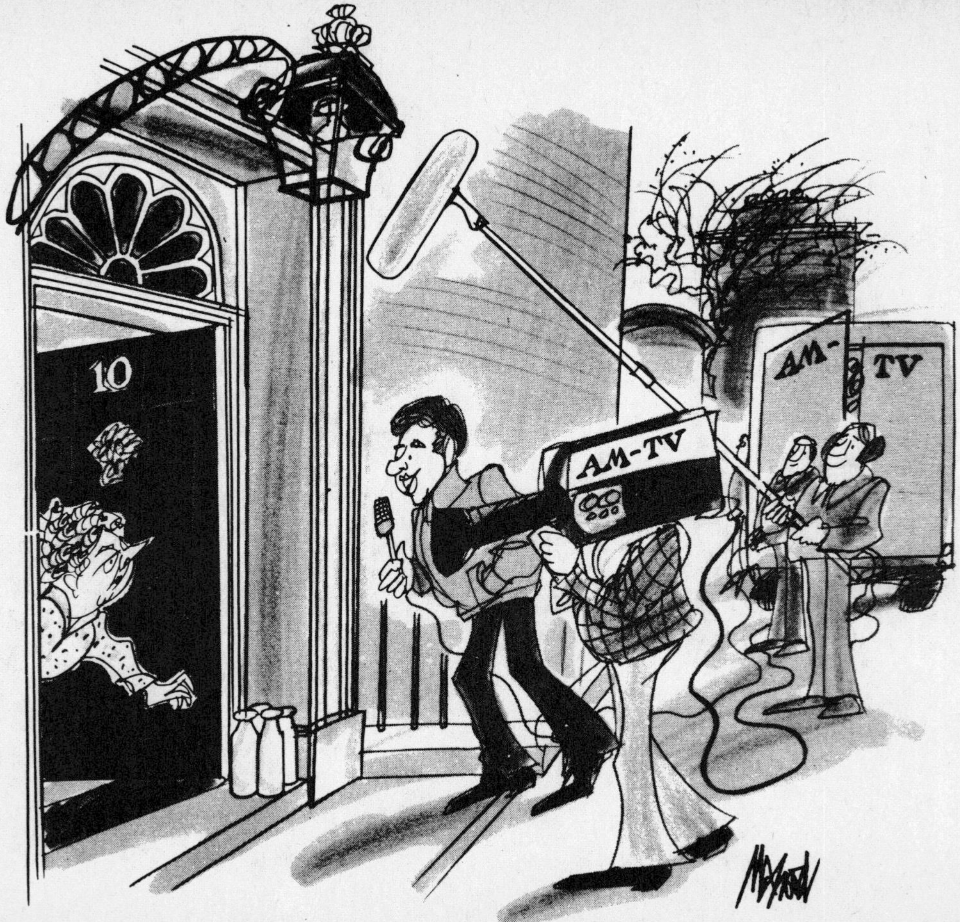

"... and now, live from No 10..."